WHAT WOULD GRANNY SAY?

And Other Somewhat Embellished Memories

By the Rev. Tony Rowell

South Carolina United Methodist Advocate Press

To Patti,
In Christ,
Tony

First published in the United States of America in 2020
by the South Carolina United Methodist Advocate Press.

Library of Congress Cataloging-in-Publication Data
Rowell, Anthony S.
What Would Granny Say, and Other Somewhat Embellished Memories
p. cm.
Includes bibliographical reference

Cover photo: *Peaceful Walkway*, by Tony Rowell

ISBN 978-0-9854721-4-6

At the time of this writing, there are about 7.8 billion people on this planet, and I can only think of one who would put up with me for very long. God blessed me many years ago with my lovely bride, Mary, and it is to her that I dedicate this book. She was my high school sweetheart and remains my sweetheart to this day, forty-some-odd years later. God has blessed me real good.

—Tony Rowell

Table of Contents

Introduction

Old memories are odd things, aren't they? They're kind of like mental cicadas. They can lay dormant for years, and then one day they crawl out from the mud of your mind, climb up your brain stem, shake off their tired old skins, and take flight.

Now, most memories head off to find better accommodations and you never see them again, but every now and then, one decides to hang around. That darn thing will find a cozy spot in a quiet corner of your mind, set up housekeeping, and then start humming one of those incessant tunes that ricochets around the inside of your skull looking for a way out. If you don't tend to it quickly, the volume will rise and an echo will form, and before long, your memory has gone to seed.

Then you'll find yourself dreaming about that old memory, but now unicorns and fairy sprites are dancing and prancing around the old homeplace in your mind, and that just won't do.

This little collection of essays or stories, or whatever you decide they are, is my attempt at preventing my memories and other considerations from getting too far out of hand.

My prayer is that you will enjoy reading them as much as I enjoyed liberating them.

Oh, yeah, I hope you don't mind, but there might be a little wannabe philosopher stuff in there, too, but not much. I promise.

The author as a young boy.

—*Tony Rowell*

Study of an Outhouse, by Tony Rowell

Prada and Presence

I have never cared for neckties. Of all the clothing in my closet, only the necktie has nefarious intent when it comes to my personal well-being.

My shoes and socks protect my feet from the pebbles of life. My shirts and pants protect me from the elements, as well as from embarrassment. The older I become, the more I appreciate clothing. Even my underwear wards off chafing, while the noble hat sheds rain and protects my noggin from the rays that would do me harm. The entire ensemble is there to protect my person and give me style—everything that is, save the necktie.

I would be reticent to meet a mind so twisted as the one that first tied a hangman's noose around a man's neck and called it fashion. To say such an action was merely passive aggressive is a gross understatement. This is just a wild guess, but I believe the individual guilty of such an odious act just may have had a problem with men.

My mother liked ties. My father, like Adam before him, dutifully wore the things with a smile on his face and a "yes, ma'am" on his lips. In me, however, that pairing produced a Cain of sorts. From an early age I kicked and bucked when the reins were placed on my neck. I have always hated the things. Perhaps like Cain before me, I consider them to be a mark of subservience.

That being said, as a kid I was indeed subservient to my mother; that was back before the inmates took over the asylum, so I wore ties to church most every Sunday. A nice little clip-on job as a rule, but when Mom was filled with evil intent and determined to punish her little Cain for his sins, real and imagined, she would bring out the dreaded bowtie. It was usually a light blue or green plaid.

I remember the last time I wore one of those things. I was seven years of age or so, as I recall. It was early Sunday morning in Panama City, Florida, mid-July and hot as blazes. My Granny Tharpe was on edge, borderline frantic and not to be messed with. She had just spent a good thirty minutes wrestling with a seven-year-old, and as I stood there dressed to the nines replete with patent leather shoes and a light green bowtie, she thought she had me cowed. So she gave me a stern look and said, "You stand right there. Don't move. I'll be right back." She then went out to take care of her own ablutions and other preparations for Sunday service.

Well, while she was otherwise occupied, I took the opportunity to go out back and dig for worms under the catawba tree. I reasoned that Wednesday was on the way, the mullet were running hot and heavy, and you can never be too prepared for fishing.

Even Granny knew when she was beaten. When she found me, instead of wearing me out like I deserved, she just started laughing—one of those old satisfying deep belly laughs that were her hallmark.

When she finally caught her breath, she told me I should be ashamed of myself, which I wasn't, took a look at her watch and, grinning, said, "Let's go!"

She brushed off what dirt she could, decided to leave my hat behind, which was crushed beyond recognition, and then she asked me where my tie was. I told her I had buried it, which was answered with a knowing grin. You see, Granny preferred dungarees to dresses any day. Then Granny, with her disorderly boy and kindred spirit in hand, headed for Saint Andrews Southern Methodist Church at a good clip to catch the first hymn.

When we arrived at church, who do you think was standing, hands on hips, on the front steps? It was my Grandmother Rowell, and she didn't share Granny's lackadaisical view of social convention. In other words, she was confounded by my appearance.

Grandmother Rowell looked at me as if I was some sort of vermin, a salamander or slug maybe, but not her grandson. I actually believe she thought I had crawled out from under a rock or something. She gave Granny, whom she considered the responsible party, a first-rate scowl, which was answered by yet another grin, and into church we all went.

Grandmother Rowell was righteously indignant. I mean, what would the town think of her grandson coming to church looking for all the world like Huck Finn? What would they think of Bill Rowell for letting his son go out in public like that? And heaven help us, what would they think of his mother? She was horrified, and I suppose rightfully so. The optics were all wrong. It didn't look good. People were going to talk. Reputations were on the line.

Granny, on the other hand, didn't care. She had managed to drag a seven-year-old cantankerous boy to church without bloodshed, and what condition he happened to be in upon arrival was of little or no consequence to her.

When Mom found out about my exploits, Granny stood between me and my just desserts in a flash of Christ-like behavior. Not only that, but she talked Mom out of making me wear a tie, bow or otherwise, from then on. The Lord gave me a jewel when he gave me my Granny.

The lesson is pretty simple in this one. Don't make excuses when it comes to the worship of your Lord and Savior. Christ doesn't care about Prada; He cares about presence. So be there.

The Picture

I have a picture I keep hanging on an inside wall of my mind. It's getting a little old now, and it's starting to fade a bit. But I keep it close by, nonetheless, so I can gaze upon it when I am feeling low or frightened or in need of direction. It is a picture of my Grandpa Tharpe.

He stands in the kitchen of Granny and Grandpa's little asbestos-sided house, which rests beside an old dirt road in the blue-collar section of Panama City, Florida. The road has since been paved, but in my mind a passing car will forever kick up dust as it heads down Drake Avenue. It's dinner time, and Granny has outdone herself because her favorite grandson has brought his best girl with him to visit all the way from South Carolina.

As I look at the picture, I notice it's getting toward dusk, but there is just enough light coming in through the window to light up Grandpa's face a bit. He leans with both his hands resting on the dinner table.

On the old table, I see a bowl of creamed corn, fresh off the cob, sitting in one of Granny's old flowery bowls with a big spoon leaned up against it ready for service. Beside the corn sits a plate full of steaming fried chicken with enough salt ingrained in the crust to cause any number of coronaries, but Lord have mercy, it sure was good. Granny has hold of a slotted spoon filled with lima beans—no, no, to Granny they were always butter beans. Nonetheless, she appears to be serving her visitor first, and Mary doesn't appear to be inclined to stand on ceremony and object. It must be summertime, because the amber of the iced tea is shimmering through the condensation on the glasses, and over behind and to the right of Grandpa, the customary chipped Pyrex dish filled with banana pudding sits on the stove tempting us with its promise of sweet coolness.

As I look up from the table, I can't help but smile when I see Grandpa's face. I see Mom in him, especially in this picture. You see, both Grandpa and Mom were given the gift of total abandonment when something or someone delighted them. I imagine in this case, Grandpa is delighted with my newfound treasure, as am I. Whatever the reason, this much I know—in his merriment he can't catch his breath. Tears are streaming down his crimson face, which is caught somewhere between a smile and a grimace as his joy is tempered with oxygen deprivation.

It was at this moment I took the picture. I didn't use a camera. I used something much more powerful. I took a snapshot with my mind, framed it, and hung it on the wall. You have no idea how much comfort that image has brought me in my life. Neither did I, until I penned this little note.

The frame is a bit tilted now, and the shine has turned to satin, but the picture remains of a man to whom I owe more than I have words to express. While my father taught me how to be strong, my Grandpa taught me gentleness. Both have served me well over the years.

But as I grow older, I pray Grandpa's gentle nature will come to the fore in my life so I can pass it on and leave a legacy of love and grace to those who follow.

As I struggled to write these words, this picture kept coming into my mind. I wondered why. Why does the Lord want me to open up my mind, to open up my soul, as it were? To be honest with you, this picture is mine. I did not want to share it.

But I know from past experience that to argue with the call of God is at one time fruitless and foolish, so share it I did.

In retrospect, perhaps there are a few lessons here.

First and foremost, cherish those you love. They are a gift of priceless value, given to you by God above. Don't take them for granted. Love them.

Second, never underestimate your value to the ones who love you. As God has given them to you, He has given you to them. God never gives a gift without a purpose behind it. Don't hide your light. Those who follow you need to see.

Finally, never forget to thank God above for the ones He has given you in your life to love. They are true living signs of His love for you.

A Fleeting Moment

I threw my right leg over the motorcycle seat and settled in. Immediately there-after, I began to question a few things, my sanity chief among them.

I also wondered if this rickety contrivance, which appeared to be held together with baling wire and prayer, would actually hold the weight of both me and the driver. Now, the driver was a slight fella with a winning smile and nerves of steel, so I knew it would carry him. After all, he had come up the hill on it. But when I sat down and heard the springs bottom out under my weight, I felt the rising of a little tickle of apprehension in the middle of my stomach.

Shortly thereafter, that tickle became a bit more intense as we careened down the mountain toward the Caribbean Sea on a road that appeared more liquid than solid, when it appeared at all. Thanks be to God, my driver was skilled, and for the most part we remained airborne, but once in a while we would return to earth, and on one such occasion we came upon a particularly ambitious hole in the ground. Shortly thereafter, my stomach was propelled into my throat while my overactive nerve center moved from my brain to the seat of my pants. That one hurt.

On top of all of this, I had nothing much to hold onto. My driver had made it clear from the beginning that hugging him and screaming like a little girl just wasn't acceptable. So I held onto the back of the seat, watched my life as it flashed before me, and kept my audible terror to a minimum.

It was about this time that I risked opening my eyes, and what I saw amazed me. Paola, a lovely young Colombian woman, my friend and contact person, was on a similar contraption right in front of me. While I was hanging on for dear life and wondering about final arrangements, she was doing her hair while watching me and grinning from ear to ear.

So much for my fearless, strong, and daring team leader facade.

Embarrassment and terror aside, little did I know that this wonderful death-defying act I was in the midst of would lead to one of the most meaningful moments in my life.

As we returned to earth for the final time and the cycle glided to a halt, a wonderful sight lay before me.

There is truly no apt way of describing the wonder of a quiet, secluded Caribbean beach. As your eyes become accustomed to the glare, your mind cannot take in all of the beauty at once. The water, as clear as crystal with just a hint of lime for color, dazzles your senses. The azure sky (I have always wanted to write that!), filled with delicate clouds and reflecting off the waves, gives the sea and the sky a turquoise hue. Where they come together is anyone's guess. Somewhere near the horizon, the sea and sky become one.

The lazy breeze traces its way through the palms, providing a counterpoint to the crashing waves, and together they sing a soothing melody that beckons the listener to find a seat and rest a while.

I had accepted the invitation, and I was doing just that—sitting with Paola on a piece of old driftwood, enjoying the peace of the place and the conversation of a good friend. We watched as little children from a nearby village played at the water's edge with the rest of our party.

In the midst of our conversation, a man of about forty, who appeared as if by magic, caught Paola's attention. He wanted a word. They spoke for a moment or two, after which she came and asked if I would be willing to go with him to offer a prayer for an ailing old man a short way down the beach. A bit aggravated at having my rest disturbed, I reluctantly followed him, accompanied by Paola, as we walked down the beach toward a little mud-sided, thatched-roof hut in the distance.

I had left my shoes back at the driftwood, forgetting the little pieces of broken coral and jagged shells that littered the ground under the palms, so it was slow-going for a while there as we picked our way forward.

Eventually, however, we arrived at the little home. It had a couple of rooms, no running water or power, no glass in the windows (another gift of the Caribbean), and it held the faint odor of persistent illness and age.

As we walked in, the heat was oppressive. Sitting in the hall on a ladderback chair was an old man, desperately trying to catch whatever breeze offered itself through the opened front door. His name was Fernando. He was 90 years of age or so, unable to speak or walk, but he had a wonderful smile and peace about him that was a tonic. His eyes, milky with age, bore no desperation, just a gentle acceptance coupled with the patience that only great age can produce. His wife, whose name escapes me, was leaning in the doorway of the little kitchen. She offered a weary but genuine smile, and her love for her husband was truly a blessing to observe.

Paola asked her what prayer was needed. She answered nothing specific, just a prayer would do.

So with Fernando's permission, I knelt down beside him and put my hand on his bare shoulder.

There have been instances in my life when I knew Christ was present, but seldom have I been so blessed as to lay my hand on his shoulder. As I prayed, the peace of Christ moved from Fernando to me, and for a moment, for a fleeting moment, I understood the peace that passes all understanding. There was nothing but that little hut, Fernando, Christ, and me.

A moment later, the breeze moved my hair and cooled my skin, and I came back, but I will never forget that moment in time when all doubt was erased and true peace was found.

I pray the same for all of you.

Fernando's House, Brisas Del Mar, Colombia, by Tony Rowell

Super Dad

When I was just a kid, about seven or eight years old as I recall, my parents decided to take the whole family on a vacation out to the Wild West. Mom and Dad sat down with a brand-new Rand McNally roadmap of the entire United States and a red marker to trace out the adventure of a lifetime. We were going to see Carlsbad Caverns, Bryce Canyon, the Painted Desert, the Grand Canyon, the Grand Tetons, the Badlands—and the apex of our trip was to be a week of camping in Yellowstone National Park.

The only problem was that the old car we had was only fit for four, not five. Since Janie, my little sister, was new on the scene, Dad had to go off and buy a brand-spanking-new 1966 Rambler Ambassador station wagon, the first car in my family to have air conditioning. We were a proud lot. Another problem lay in the fact that to make this happen, we were going to have to camp, as motels were just too expensive. So one sunny Saturday afternoon, we all loaded up in the brand new Rambler and headed to Northeast Columbia and the Holiday Camper store. We bought a little popup camper, with just enough room for five, a few supplies, and a whole host of memories. We hitched it up and were ready to go.

I have lots of stories that come from this trip, and I will probably share a few of them with you in due time, but right now let me tell you about a moment in time when my father and Superman were one and the same.

After a marvelous week of experiencing the awesome beauty of some of nature's true wonders, we arrived at Yellowstone National Park. We took a few of the obligatory tours, but my father, being an outdoorsman of sorts, preferred to do his own thing. He brought Mike, my brother, and me along as bait. We saw bears, moose, and elk. We forded streams, climbed trees, fished for trout, and cooked them over an open flame. It was truly a little boy's dream come true.

Well, one night after dark and after Mom had scooted us kids all off to bed, a park ranger came to the campsite and struck up a conversation with my father. Dad was sitting outside the camper all by himself enjoying a cup of coffee and the quiet of the evening.

Now, the walls of the camper were canvas, and since I was practicing my eavesdropping skills, I heard the ranger when he told Dad it might be a good idea for him to move inside the camper. Naturally Dad, being curious, asked why.

The ranger said there was a grizzly bear roaming the campground, and he was a big one and a little mean, so they were taking some precautions. My dad, being an outdoorsman and a man's man, didn't budge. He wasn't going to let some phantom bear interfere with his quiet time. He was the master of his domain.

Seeing that Dad was going to hold fast to his position, the ranger got up to leave and told him to just keep an eye out and be careful. Dad said he sure would, and then he casually asked the ranger where he thought this particular bear might be.

Well, to the best of my recollection, the ranger pointed a little to the right of the camper and told Dad the bear was off in that direction about, oh, fifty feet or so.

It was at that moment in time when my father and Superman became one—because without the aid of a jet pack, propeller, or even a phone booth, my father flew.

I can still feel the camper quake. I can still hear the crashing sound as my father, a normally sane and measured human being, leapt with the agility of a jungle cat from his chair to the inside of that little camper. It was truly an impressive sight. From a seated position he covered that considerable distance and never once touched the ground.

The ranger stared after him, fascinated for a moment, but he eventually came to himself and headed off once again to warn other folks of the imminent danger. His warnings, however, stood in stark contrast to the somewhat derisive, cackling laughter issuing from our camper and filling the night air.

My mother was beside herself with joy, an uproarious joy she saved only for special occasions, and my father making a fool of himself was pretty special in her estimation. Prudence dictated that we kids feign sleep, but there were delighted grins all around.

In the end my father, now deflated and somewhat ashamed, slunk off to bed to dream of slaying dragons and of better days to come.

1 Peter 5:8-9a says, "Your enemy the devil prowls around like a roaring lion looking for someone to devour. Resist him, standing firm in the faith" (NIV).

But remember to avoid him as much as possible, and never let pride trap you in his grasp. There is a time to run!

Roving, Rolling, Angry Thunder
Haiti, January 2010

In my dream state, I could see it moving from one mountain ridge to another and back again. It crested a small hill a mile or so away, then disappeared into the shadow of a valley, only to reappear once again, slipping and skipping across a small lake shimmering silver in the moonlight. The water rippled as it passed over, but like dust behind a pickup on a dry dirt road, it quickly settled and came to rest once again, at peace. For a time, the darkness vanished, and in my dream I prayed it would not return. My prayers were in vain, however, for return it did—and this time it was much closer than before. Over to my left I saw, or rather sensed, the apparition. The mounting growl of furious thunder in the distance heralded its coming.

As is so often true in dreams, I tried to run, for by now escape was all I longed for. But my legs refused to answer. I remember hearing my panting breath as I desperately tried to crawl away from the approaching danger, but I was in quicksand and trapped.

The terrifying sound drew closer. I could feel it behind me. It roared in my ears. The taste of fear was on my tongue when something flashed in my mind: a memory, a thought, a word, reality.

"You can hear it coming!" he said.

"What was that?" I asked.

"You can hear it coming!" he repeated.

"What?" I said, still confused.

"The quake, the quake! You can hear it before it hits! Roving, rolling, angry thunder—that's the sound to listen for."

I awoke to the sound of ten thousand terrified voices crying out "Jesus!" in perfect unison.

The quake had thrown me from my cot to the floor. Shattered floor tiles were all around me, and bits of plaster and mortar were raining down from the ceiling above, as the thunder rolled away to the west and the echo of the desperate cry faded.

As the morning dawned on Port-au-Prince, it found a man with a changed perspective on life and on himself. The feeling of insignificance and helpless fear of the night before had a profound effect on me. Before that moment, I had felt in control. I was, after all, an intelligent, spiritually mature, physically capable man, and I truly believed that I could take care of myself, not only physically, but also spiritually.

But as I crouched, terrified, beneath that flimsy cot and prayed the ceiling above me would hold, I realized I was absolutely helpless before the awesome power of nature and completely at the mercy of the awesome power of my God.

It has taken awhile, but I have reconciled myself to those facts. And while the power of nature still demands my respect, the power of God Almighty is what I cling to for hope and assurance.

For you see, I understand good construction techniques and happenstance kept the ceiling from falling that night. Another strong aftershock or a stiff breeze could have easily ended my earthly existence, for I neither demand nor expect more protection than the many who lost their lives in the big quake a few days before.

Nature, you see, promises nothing. Her whims are unpredictable and her moods uncharted. But God Almighty, Jesus Christ, is a God of stability and strength. He never varies, and He never fails.

I will never forget the wonderful sound of my Savior's name echoing through the night all those years ago in Haiti. I will also never forget my surprise when I realized that I, too, had joined in the cry. Like so many others that night, when terror overtook me, I cried out to the only one I knew who could help.

I now realize in a real way that He, Christ, will never leave me. I realize that no matter the outcome, Christ would have never left me that night, and He will never leave me now. His promises hold true.

Count on that. No matter what you may be going through, He is always there! He is faithful and true. He will never leave you.

Haitian Earthquake 2010, by Tony Rowell

The Old House

The old door was slightly askew, and the window panes had long since fallen victim to young boys with mischief on their minds. But right in the middle of the lower panel was nailed a piece of plywood, cut in the shape of a heart and painted blue. Now that heart was the only thing left that had any paint visible. The rest of the house, what was still standing, had long since lost its color.

That heart nailed to that old rickety door captured my imagination. I wanted to know more about the folks who'd nailed it there. So I turned around and pulled into the old overgrown drive.

There were no "No Trespassing" or "Beware of Dog" signs, so I got out of the truck, grabbed my camera from the passenger's seat, and made my way through the tall, sweet grass to the door.

I wanted to see what pictures could be had, but more than that, I wanted to try to reconstruct the family who had lived there. Have you ever done that sort of thing, or is it just me?

As I approached the old place, I saw through one of the empty panes that a calendar was tacked on the wall dated 1973, so it had been a long time since anyone, save squatters, had been in this old house. That would make it thirty-five some-odd years since the old house had been occupied on a regular basis. It is amazing what was still left.

I decided to take a few photographs. I had been working on my still-life and black-and-white shooting, and this place was perfect. So I gingerly stepped up on the old front porch and peered through the window to the right of the door. I didn't go inside. That would be rude, and besides, just stepping on the front porch was the biggest step of faith I had taken all week. So I just looked through the broken windows feeling a little ashamed of myself for prying.

I first noticed something that interested me, or at least the incongruity of it interested me. I noticed, as I looked through the camera lens, that on the inside of the bedroom door there were posters of Billy Graham and Bob Jones and all sorts of other evangelists tacked up. They were yellowing and the edges were curled, but you could see Billy was still young and Bob had his hair swept back, just like a good evangelist of old ought. There was a crusade heading for Atlanta.

In the middle of all the preachers, there was a pencil drawing of Jesus with his head bowed in prayer. It was an impressive piece of artwork, to tell the truth. That door was something to behold. It was a simple yet elegant and rickety shrine to the Lord and Savior of the occupants.

Then I panned over from the door to an old dresser with one leg sticking through the floor that made it lean just a little to the front and a bit to the left. On top of that dresser was the finest collection of empty whiskey bottles I have ever seen. I don't know, maybe a squatter did the drinking, but the pictures of Christ and all those whiskey bottles in the same room kind of encompassed the human condition to my way of thinking. There was temptation, there was sin, and there was Christ kneeling in prayer for the sinner. Poignant picture, if you ask me.

Then I got a further bit of insight into the man of the house. Over on the floor next to the Jesus door was an old Zebco 33 fishing reel, the old metal type I used when I was a kid. It didn't have a rod. It was just the old rusted-out reel, and it put me in mind of my Grandpa Tharpe. I don't know why, but I liked the man of the house after seeing that, even if he was a drunkard.

Next I went to what was left of the kitchen. I had a pretty good picture of the man of the house. He was just a bit conflicted, I figure, but I wanted to get to know his wife. Call me a sexist if you want, but I figured the best way to get to know the lady of the house was to go to the kitchen.

All the windowpanes in the kitchen were long since gone, as well, so it was easy to see the old faded green ceramic duck sitting on the weather-worn sill. My Granny used to have that same duck on a shelf in the kitchen. Actually, she had a flock. I have one of them over in my office. I liked the lady of the house instinctively.

The present duck was broken up a bit. You could tell, though, that at one time it had an open back so you could plant a flower in it, so I figured the woman liked to keep her realm pretty and fresh.

She also cooked like my Granny, if the five empty cans of Crisco scattered on the floor were any indication. She liked the finer things, too, in spite of her station in life, because somehow a silver spoon—a real silver spoon—had survived the years and rested on the window sill just out of sight behind the duck.

There is a lot more to be said about her, but I will leave that for another day. Suffice it to say, I would have liked her had we met in this life.

By the way, the 1973 calendar hanging on the kitchen wall was opened to November. One of her kids had a birthday on the seventh, and the whole crowd was coming over for Thanksgiving, if the star and smiley face were any indication. I hope they all made it.

Finally, I went to the living room. There was an old couch, or what was left of it. The windows were all consistent in their brokenness, and the various angles of the window and door frames gave the room a Picasso flavor. The old plaster was peeling off the walls and dripping from the ceiling. There was an ancient fireplace with a beat-up mantle in front of the couch.

And sitting on the couch, much to my surprise, was a rather large, elderly teddy bear. For the life of me it appeared as if the teddy bear was looking over at the mantle remembering what pictures used to rest there and thinking of days gone by.

As I returned to my truck, I got to thinking that the remnants of a family remain long after they have gone, and they tell a lot.

Then I realized that one of these days someone is going to be walking down what appears to be an old overgrown path just off of Beechwoods Drive a bit outside of Lexington, and at the end of the path they are going to come across an old derelict log house with the windows all busted out, sitting slightly askew on its foundation, with beams wavering. The vines will have overtaken it by then, because nature always reclaims her own. Then that someone will say to themselves, "I wonder who lived here and what they were like?"

I would be very interested in finding out what they discover. Will they find remnants worthy of a child of God or the leftovers of a life spent on selfish pursuits? I pray the former, but I fear the latter. How about you?

Mullet Hunting

The freshwater mullet is an elusive adversary. He is at one time as crafty as a fox and as dumb as a doorknob. He is adventurous and cowardly. He longs to try new things, and yet is afraid to follow through. He swims the current with glee and leaps with fear from a smooth lake. He is an enigma, a mystery, and a fine meal.

Years ago, when just a young boy, I used to hunt this famed creature with a fervor seldom rivaled to this day. I would spend hours on end, shirtlessly, shoelessly, and carelessly following a pack or school of mullet up and down the dam that spanned the Dead Lakes in my boyhood haunt of Wewahitchka, Florida.

You see, the technique for winning this prize isn't complicated, but it must be carried off with great precision and a dedication so intense it borders on fanaticism.

The mullet spend their day on the smooth side of the spillway, which drops the overflow of the Dead Lakes back into the Chipola River. On the drop-off side, the water is rough, and large boulders have been placed there to prevent erosion. Largemouth bass love this area mainly because any little fish that comes over the top is bruised and battered and just a bit confused when it lands in the rapids—and thus is an easy meal.

The smooth side is just that. It is where the water banks up just before it overflows, and the resulting water up against the spillway is an eddy of sorts. The current just under the surface is strong enough to host a veritable parade of trash for the mullet to eat but not strong enough to pull them over the top, but Lord help the mullet that ventures too close to the surface. He has a wild ride ahead of him.

That being said, the mullet swim as a pack up and down the spillway just below the strong current all day long, catching whatever bits of garbage come their way, and it is this tendency to bite first and taste later that gives the hunter the advantage, small as it is.

With a stout cane pole, a strong hook, and the patience of Job mixed with the fortitude of Sisyphus, a young boy can bring home the bacon, if the conditions are just right. You have to lean over the rail, so you have the proper leverage when the time comes, and lower your hook, baited with just a tad of wriggler, about four or five feet in front of the oncoming herd of mullet. The difficult part is not spooking them, number one, and determining the correct depth, number two. Oh, I almost forgot—not falling in is actually the first most difficult thing.

When you get it just right, the lead mullet will sidle up to your worm, give it a noncommittal glance, and then, with an imperceptible intake of water, make the worm disappear as if by magic, only to make it reappear a millisecond later when he or she has determined that it isn't trashy enough to eat.

It is only the hunter with the sharpest focus and lightning-fast reflexes that gains the prize. For when fishing for mullet, your focus must be razor sharp. Nothing in the world exists but that lead mullet before you. You have to get into the mind of the mullet, and when you are in the zone, you unconsciously and imperceptibly intake air at the precise moment when that worm disappears.

With that unconscious intake of air, your body springs into action with a precision and speed that defies logic and physiology, and with seemingly one movement, that mullet is airborne.

Up he rises from the water. He performs a perfect arch above your head and then comes crashing down on the pavement behind you. That is, of course, if there is pavement behind you.

At eight years of age, my power of focus was quite acute.

One afternoon, in the mid-summer as I recall, I was hunting for mullet. I was in the zone. No mullet was safe that day. I had already sent several to the icebox, and I knew the time to head back to Panama City was closing in, so my focus heightened all the more.

As the sun began to set, the final school was before me, and the lead mullet was magnificent. As the yellow sun shown off of the silver scales, the effect was dazzling. The fine head, the graceful lines; I was mesmerized.

I had to have that prize.

So with a skill borne from years of practice, I lowered the perfect morsel before the intended victim, and with the now-accustomed mutual intake of air and water, the magic happened.

That beauty was lifted from the water, sailed through the air with a style to be envied by all, disappeared over my left shoulder in the setting sun's glare, and came crashing down with the customary thud. Or was that a crash?

My exultation at having gained such a prize was quickly tempered. For when I turned around, I saw that my newfound trophy was beautifully displayed on the hood of the local game warden's pickup truck. Right there, in a mullet-shaped indentation, lay my fish.

It turns out that it doesn't take all that long for an eight-year-old's life to flash before his eyes.

I will dispense with the rest of the story for now. Suffice it to say, it ain't all that pretty. I'll tell you this, though. I believe my feelings at that precise moment would best be described as mixed.

I felt compelled to tell you this story, but the reason for the telling remains unknown to me. Perhaps, like me, the Lord simply enjoys reliving those simple, innocent times. Perhaps there is some deep theological meaning hidden within the interplay between mullet, current, bait, and boy, or perhaps not.

One way or the other, I pray the reading brought a smile to your face, a pleasant memory to your mind, a bit of rest for your heart, and some peace to your soul.

Grandpa Tharpe at Willis Landing

Taste and See

"How can you eat with those things?" I asked.

"What things?" he queried.

"Those hands. They are nasty. Why don't you go give them a wash before you sit down to eat dinner? There are ladies present."

Granny laughed at that, but technically she was a lady, and a grand one at that, and sitting alongside Granny was Joan, my Native American kin. I could never figure out the relation, but I know there was one because everybody told me there was.

Joan had the definite air of a lady about her: early forties, proud and reserved, and beautiful to boot. She was part of the trio from the old green house across the street, John, Joan, and Jenny respectively. Jenny was a step or two younger than me, Joan was her momma, and John Deal was her daddy.

It was forty some-odd years ago, and I was sitting in Granny's old kitchen staring at John over a plate of fried chicken, field peas, and hoecake. His hands were all black lines and dirty fingernails, and standing out in relief against the glass of iced tea he held, they looked a little dangerous to me. So being the spontaneous teenager I was, I blurted out my objection.

John laughed. "Son, I have been washing these hands for over forty years, and this is as clean as they get. When you work in grease, it becomes part of you."

And it surely had. On closer inspection, his hands had a gray look to them, and the little lines running hither and thither looked like a map of one of the blackwater river systems in Florida's panhandle. I can't even begin to describe the fingernails, but he was right. All evidence to the contrary, they were clean. At least, nothing had rubbed off on the hoecake he was eating.

John grinned at me and held out his hands, palms up. With the dark lines running every which-a-way, they looked for all the world like a road map. The road map of a blue-collar life.

As it turns out, John was right about the cleanliness. He died a few years ago of a heart attack, not the ptomaine poisoning I figured would get him.

Those old marked-up hands of John's came to mind the other day when Mary and I stepped into a dilapidated old building painted like a carnival ride to eat lunch. We were down in Charleston, and Mary had read of Martha Lou's Kitchen, and we decided to give it a try.

There is a mystical moment experienced twice a day on the waterways of the coast. It rests in between the tides. For a twinkling all is calm. The waters are still for an instant, the world is at rest, and then the relentless pull of the moon heaves the water in another direction. The magic spell is broken, and movement begins once again.

Martha Lou's stands on that mystical spot in Charleston. On one side the tourists, the hustle and bustle, and the noise of commerce, and on the other side the everyday lives of the locals. In between stands Martha Lou's, caring for both with equal care, genuine friendliness, and old-timey eating.

As Mary and I settled down into our mismatched chairs, the cool feel of the aged Formica tabletop was somehow comforting. I gazed around at what had to have been an old porch at one time in its life, but now it was closed in and filled with six or seven tables, chairs of all shapes and sizes, and tablecloths from different eras, if my guess is right. The walls were covered with family photos, many faded with age and spotted with who knows what. The atmosphere was filled with the aroma of what can only be described as Granny's old kitchen.

There was a hint, almost a mist, of Crisco in the air. Not the oil, but the white kind from the can. Floating within the mist rested the afterglow of chicken and fish and some wonderfully mysterious something that had lain for a brief moment in the fryer. Cabbage and collards finished the symphony. Oh, there were other instruments, other aromas scattered about, but they all played second fiddle to the fryer, the cabbage, and the collards.

I don't know about you, but for me, some foods taste better in a place that has been around long enough to have some grease up under its fingernails. I like to eat in a place that has seen something, not just heard about it. Martha Lou's has seen some things.

As Mary's hair danced in the box fan's stream, I gazed down at an old galvanized pipe running along the wall beside our table. It had to be galvanized because it had enough layers of paint on it to go back to the years before PVC. I followed it as it traced its path, turning this way and that into the kitchen. It reminded me of the lines on John's palm, and I got to wishing that old pipe could talk.

There was a young couple there. They looked like newlyweds. At least they were friendly enough to be newlyweds, and for some reason, impetuous youth I suppose, they had stopped into this little rundown place for a bite.

I bet they left with a memory.

When our food arrived, I was taken back to my Granny's kitchen, and the memories flowed through my mind like a gentle stream. I felt comforted somehow. That old feeling of being safely wrapped in the family fold tugged at me.

I hated leaving that place. It made me feel good.

I figure there is a lesson in there somewhere. Perhaps it is as simple as remembering that for one person the past brings comfort, and for another the past brings discovery. For one person the old ways resurrect memories of the past, and for another revisiting the old ways produces memories for the future.

It seems as of late many within the church of Jesus Christ have decided the past is of no use and only the future has value. Some have decided the truths of our forefathers, the traditions of the family, and the old ways are simply stains that must be scrubbed away with new thought and new theology.

What many fail to understand is that the old ways, the old traditions and truths, are maps that trace the way from the cross of Jesus Christ to where we find ourselves today. To ignore them, to discount them, to offhandedly declare them relics of little use, is to display imprudence at the very least. To cast them aside is to lose one's compass and direction.

The old and the new are not necessarily mutually exclusive. They can sit side by side and enjoy the same meal, one for comfort and rest and one for discovery and zest. The key is to sit down together and enjoy the meal.

"Taste and see that the Lord is good; blessed is the man who takes refuge in Him" (Psalm 34:8 NIV).

Latvian Profesor, by Tony Rowell

Targeted

It was mid-morning in mid-July. It promised to be one of those days when the humidity and temperature merge together to produce just a hint of brimstone in the air. I was sitting with my brother, Mike, in an old rented wooden jon boat with an anchor at one end and an empty bait can at the other for bailing purposes. We had found ourselves the shade of a big cypress and settled there.

Mike was somewhere around ten years old, and I was a few years behind him. As we sat there, a couple of cane poles apiece resting on the gunwales and our bobbers fanned out in several directions, we both silently prayed that nothing would bite. Neither of us wanted to move. Even at that young age the heat of the day had drained us, the shade had called us, and our lids were heavy and working their way toward closed.

Now, my Granny Tharpe and Grandma Rowell were sharing another boat and had hit upon a bream bed a little ways down the river from us. They had tied off a bit from the bank to get a better shot at it, and they ended up sitting in the full sun. You see, when you come upon a bream bed, even the heat of Satan's breath will not deter a true fisherman—or a couple of fisherwomen, in this case. There is nothing like a bunch of biting fish to bring a blue-blooded socialite and blue-collared Rosie Riveter together. They both had on their heads one of those pointy straw hats that gave just a hint of Far Eastern mystique, and I think it was the hats that caught the attention of the young pilot out for the day from Eglin Air Force Base.

You see, down around the Chipola River it's mostly catfish and cottonmouths, and the Air Force folks practice down there so as to not kill any civilians on the off-chance that something goes wrong.

Being a well-trained pilot, he came in from the east with the sun behind him. Mike and I had heard him. Being little boys, we were fascinated by anything fast, so the far-off sound caught our ears.

But Granny and Grandma were so focused on the fish that the muted noise of the jet engine blended in with the cicadas all around them and went unnoticed.

Our young eyes quickly located the gleaming jet fighter as it dropped like a falcon from the sky and settled a few feet above the trees downrange. Fascinated, we watched as the pilot approached our position. When he reached the river a mile or so below us, the young hotshot truly began to feel his oats and dropped just below the tree line, for all intents and purposes like a rock skipping on the surface of the river.

It was an impressive display of prowess made all the more exciting by the fact that my Granny and my Grandma, the intended targets, remained unaware.

He barreled down the river with deadly focus and pinpoint precision with his affections set upon the two old ladies. At the last moment I could almost hear his maniacal laughter as he pulled up and disappeared into the morning sky.

First came the shadow. When the shadow passed over the target, both Grandmas responded the same. They responded just like a rabbit would should the shadow of an owl traveling at Mach 1 pass over. They had just enough time to blink and begin their instinctive crouch when the shadow was quickly followed by the sonic boom, which was quickly followed by thoughts of the coming rapture accompanied by straw hats, cane poles, crickets, and a few choice words being lifted into the air and scattered over the waters.

Mike and I were beside ourselves with excitement, joy, and laughter. You don't see something like that every day, and besides, we revered anyone who could get the better of Granny Tharpe.

Granny Tharpe's response was predictable for her. When her color finally returned, she responded with her trademark cackle of excitement at the rush received from the sudden fear. Grandma Rowell's response was a bit more surprising to me. Apparently, her blue blood went white and, along with it, her proper language went south. Trust me, that young whippersnapper got a world-class tongue-lashing, and I learned a few new words that morning myself.

Now to tell the truth, I don't know which gave Granny Tharpe more pleasure: the excitement of being targeted or the satisfaction of witnessing Grandma Rowell unravel. If I had to take bets, I would back the unraveling any day.

I'll bet you're wondering why I wrote of this old memory of mine. I'll tell you. It could be a lesson on how to respond to the surprises of life, or it could be a lesson on the human being and the accompanying frailties that lie just beneath the calm facade of us all, but it's not. I just thought that you might need a minute's rest from the worries of your world today. The Lord knows that we all do from time to time.

Reunion

The family reunion is something that seems to be slowly fading away, and that is a crying shame, if you ask me. Far too few people have any idea of the stock from which they sprang, and in turn they don't know of the strength and weakness, of the glory and tragedy that flows through their veins.

I happen to think we are made less when an ignorance of the past holds sway in our lives as individuals and as a society. To my way of thinking, we need the strength of the family, and in order for that strength to be passed on, contact needs to be re-established from time to time.

Shared remembrances are treasures of which few know their true value.

Years ago when I was a boy, I remember looking forward to the Jenkins Family Reunion every June. Jenkins was my Granny Tharpe's maiden name, and every June the entire tribe would come together at one of the three Jenkins kids' homes for a covered-dish dinner under the trees followed by an afternoon of loud voices, oft-told stories, and screaming children. It was a wonderful mess, as my Grandpa used to say.

When the reunion was to be held at my Granny's house, the excitement was muted a little by the fact that the adventure of the affair would suffer from familiarity. When it was to be held at Aunt Nellie's, the fun was often dampened by the brooding visage of Uncle Howard. Uncle Howard wasn't a hard man by any means, but to a boy, he was a bit too quiet and a bit too dark, and a certain foreboding drifted on the air when he was near. Now admittedly, Uncle Howard's shadow was pierced by the brightness of Aunt Nellie's gold front tooth and her laughing nature, but it remained as a sort of uncomfortable mist that worked its way into a child's mind as the day grew longer.

All of that aside, once every three years we would all climb into whatever flavor station wagon was available and head off to Crestview, Florida, to Uncle Shine and Aunt Addie's house, and have ourselves a great time. There was just something about that place that shouted freedom and family, and I cannot remember a time when I didn't have a ball there.

Uncle Shine had coon dogs and chickens and all sorts of other things that could keep a young boy's interest through the day, and when interest in such things finally began to wane, Uncle Shine's backyard came complete with a poor man's amusement park.

You see, Uncle Shine worked for the phone company, and he couldn't resist taking home all the empty wooden spools he could find. I figure he had in mind grand projects he would do with them, but they mostly just stayed out back next to the pasture fence. It was a tribute to the patience of Aunt Addie that he had such a collection of giant bobbins decorating the backyard.

Well, Aunt Addie's burden was a delight to all of us kids. We would turn those spools up on their sides, climb up on them, and walk-roll them all over the yard. We would hold races all morning. We would fall off, bust our rear ends, brush off, and have at it again all day long while the old folks sat around and talked of old times, one another, and the occasional innocent bystander.

When dinnertime came, we would all climb down reluctantly, crestfallen and defeated, knowing we would have to sit still and quiet with the old folks for a while. Our sorrow, however, was short-lived, for as the wonderful smells reached our nostrils, the grief at leaving our play was replaced with an urgency borne of a ravenous hunger. We would stampede over to the tables and fill our plates with some of the best home-cooking that ever came off a stove, and sit in and amongst the grownups and listen. For you see, at that time in our history, the phrase, "a child is to be seen and not heard" had not been totally expunged from the social lexicon.

It was during this time of listening—the time when family stories were told, embellished a bit, and told again—that the familial DNA was passed from one generation to another.

It was then that I learned of my family's Native American history. It was then that I learned of the magic my Great-Grandpa Jenkins could perform with a hammer, a level, a handsaw, and a few sticks of lumber. It was then that I learned of my quiet grandpa's deadly rage when my mother was threatened as a child. It was then when I learned of the abject poverty from which my mother emerged. It was then that I learned of myself. It was then that I learned I was part of something greater than myself.

I was part of the family.

We all need that, I think. We all need to know we are part of something greater than ourselves. Whether it's a particular branch on the Jenkins family tree or the family of God, the human being needs to have connection, for without such connection, the human fruit withers on the vine.

With the advent of social networking websites, it seems human connection is rapidly being replaced with the cold keys of the keyboard and the inanimate face of the monitor.

To my way of thinking, there is great danger in this. As family structures teeter under the weight of daily stress, tightly woven familial fiber is needed to hold them together. As society wavers under the stress of economic, moral, and spiritual meltdown, it is the families joined together with shared beliefs, shared struggles, and shared histories that will allow society to stand firm. As the church of God reels amidst attacks from without and within, as the moral truths of the scriptures are assailed, as the Word of God is parsed to suit our rebellious and sinful ways, as Christ's holy name is taken from the public arena, it is through the power of Christ, bolstered by the shared strength of the people of God, that the church will stand.

My challenge to each of you is to let nothing sever your connection with Christ and His people, for nothing is of more importance. You are part of something greater than yourself. You are part of the family of God, and that family suffers in your absence.

Aunt Nellie, Uncle Shine and Granny Tharpe

An Apple for the Teacher

He was maybe six years old, seven at the most. He appeared to be somewhere in the middle of my grandchildren, age-wise at least. And he was looking at me in the most curious fashion. Not overly interested necessarily, but slightly aggravated and a little sympathetic almost to the point of pity.

I think his young mind was trying to figure out where on the evolutionary scale a man who didn't know the proper way to pick up apples should be placed. Cap this with the fact that I didn't understand Latvian, which rendered me speechless in his presence, and I figure he figured I came from an altogether different branch of the tree than he. Much to his relief, I might add.

I was down on one knee under an apple tree in the high, damp grass surrounding Camp Wesley at the apple festival. Camp Wesley is a Methodist youth camp just outside of Liepāja, Latvia. It is beautifully situated on twenty or so acres of pristine farmland that smells of newly turned earth and fresh-mown hay. I have always found those two fragrances soothing and a little heady. It's my kinda place. Add a gentle breeze and the everlasting wwohh, wwohh, wwohh of the nearby windmills, and a hammock comes to mind every time ... but I digress.

I was on my knees, picking up apples, and thinking of how ingenious Anita was for calling a workday a festival when this young boy comes up and does his best to pull me to my feet. I think he was concerned for my britches, which were quickly becoming soaked and soiled. He was a born professor, and he wanted to teach me how to do this thing properly.

First he tried to tell me what to do, but my sorrowful expression and blank eyes only confirmed his initial impression of me. So after determining I was verbally challenged, he tried pantomime. In that most of the apples were on the ground because of a storm, he proceeded to demonstrate, in a slow and extremely exaggerated manner, the correct way to stand up straight, bend at the waist, extend your arm, pick up an apple, and gently place it in the sack. He showed me twice, so I could get it.

In essence, he was saying, "They're just apples, Sir. There is no need to bow down to them. Just pick 'em up like a normal human being." He was very patient and just a little condescending.

What he didn't know was had I attempted his method of picking up apples, I would have quickly become nothing more than an oversized piece of yard-art with my head planted in the grass and my rear-end pointing skyward, never to move again.

At his age I may well have bent that way, but at my age it ain't happening. Well, it isn't the age so much as the mileage, but the result would have been the same.

So with great concentration I watched him twice, smiled, and then got back down on my knees. His expression was priceless: "Yep, from a different branch of the tree than me," with an implied, "Thank God Almighty."

He wandered off shaking his head from side to side, thanking the Lord for his pedigree, and wondering about mine.

Well after some effort, with soaked and soiled britches, I finally filled up my sack and stood up to carry it back to the barn for processing. You know, a good-sized burlap sack filled with small apples is surprisingly heavy. So I was half carrying, half dragging this sack when I noticed a slight, but perceptible lessening of the weight.

I looked down and my young professor had dropped his regal robes and was doing his best to carry the other side of the sack for me. His eyes said, "Sir, I might not be able to do anything about where you came from or how you do things, but I will do my best to lighten your load."

We made it to the cutting table and dropped the sack. Then he took my hand and led me to one of the older church ladies from Tasi for safekeeping. He didn't want me to hurt myself.

There was a brief conversation, and I can only figure that the matriarch told the young'un who and what I was, because his expression immediately changed from compassion for me to a combination of concern for the team and childlike wonder at the vagaries of life. I watched him amble off and thought to myself, "Somebody is raising that child right."

Later that day I watched as he taught David how to put apple pieces in a grinder. He seemed well satisfied with David as a student. David acted like he had some sense, at least.

The Lord gives me these stories to tell, and sometimes I wonder why. Not this time. This time the message is simple, essential, and poignant.

In a world, in a church, that seems bent on self-destruction through a focus on self to the exclusion of all, this little professor taught a simple and golden truth: kindness before judgment, love before rancor, others before self, and Christ above all.

No Excuses

When I was a young boy and spent much of my time down on the panhandle of Florida with my Granny and Grandpa Tharpe, there was one woman who fascinated me—and of whom I was scared half to death. No, it wasn't my Granny; I was in awe of her. It was Granny's next-door neighbor. Her name was Irene, and she lived in a little house to the left of Granny's, if you were facing the place.

While Granny's house was light and airy, Irene's place was a dark affair. It had live oaks festooned with Spanish moss overhanging the front porch. Wisteria vines clung to the railings and worked their way up the cypress and catawba trees, which shaded the rest of the house. Old tar-laced roll roofing acted as siding so the house was a motley combination of brown paper and black tar, and the yard was in a perpetual state of disarray.

I don't know why she scared me so. Perhaps it was the sheer size of the woman, or the evil glare from underneath those seldom-washed black bangs of hers, or maybe it was the voice that sounded like a broom should be under it. But one way or the other, I avoided her like the plague.

Nonetheless, I was a little boy and apt to be mischievous and a bit restless, as most little boys tend to be. In that there were no video games back then to occupy my time and no Ritalin to quell my urges, I tended to get into a bit of trouble from time to time. That being said, I usually had some help.

You see, I have a second cousin by the name of Scott, and back then he had a gift for coming up with devious things to do and having someone else do them. In that I enjoyed his company, the role of someone else often fell to me.

One late summer Sunday afternoon while the old folks were sitting around visiting, Scott and I were playing in Granny's backyard. As the afternoon wore on, interest in our normal pursuits began to fade, and we started looking for some adventure. After a while, Scott's gaze fell on the enchanted house next door, and through a double dare and the dreaded phrase "What are you scared of?" he convinced me to sneak over to Irene's house, knock on the door, and run.

Being young and stupid—at least one thing has changed since then—I decided to give it a try. So with a stealth that would make a sniper proud, I slithered through the forest of old pots, rusted car parts, and unkempt weeds without making a sound to her back door. Then I knocked, not just once but three times to prove I was immune to fear.

When I heard her heavy footsteps coming in my direction, my immunity vanished, and I turned tail and ran as fast as I could, but in the midst of my terror I somehow lost my footing, tripped over my feet, and fell headlong into her flowerbed. Lying there with a face full of forget-me-nots, I heard the back door open, caught just a whiff of sulfur on the air, and heard those hobnailed boots coming my way. My life, short as it was, flashed before my eyes.

It was then that I discovered three things. First of all, a 250-pound woman can be surprisingly swift on her feet; secondly, a seven-year-old boy can't get much traction with newly watered forget-me-nots under his feet; and finally, my second cousin could disappear faster than anybody on two feet before or since.

I will dispense with the nasty details, but I soon found myself being held by the scruff of the neck in my Granny's living room while a bunch of old ladies examined me. Most were just a bit shocked at my appearance, or maybe it was Irene's. My Granny, however, just looked at me sternly with a slight grin and I think a little gleam of admiration in her eye. She then asked for an explanation. I told her that Scott made me do it.

I will never forget her reaction. From under her grin her teeth appeared, and then from behind the teeth came a glorious belly laugh.

When she finally caught her breath, she simply said, "Scott who?"

I said, "You know, Scott my cousin."

Then she lost her smile and said, "The only Scott I see is Anthony Scott Rowell."

Somehow, I had forgotten Scott was my middle name.

I spent the rest of that day breaking the Sabbath by cleaning Irene's house from top to bottom to pay for the flowers I had destroyed, and on Monday I replanted the garden, cleaned the backyard, and mowed the grass—or what passed for grass. Scott, my cousin Scott, on the other hand, headed off to the Chipola River and spent the day fishing.

I tell this story for a couple of reasons. First and foremost, I simply enjoy reliving days gone by when things seemed to be a bit simpler, and secondly, I tell it as a bit of a warning to those of us who tend to try to cast off personal responsibility for our actions. Remember, if the road to hell is paved with good intentions, the road to nowhere is paved with excuses.

All too often the human tendency is to cast about for something or someone to blame when things don't go our way. My challenge to all of us is to look upward and inward for solutions to the challenges we face in life.

The possibilities are endless. Who knows what God has planned for your life? My prayer for you is that you allow Christ to set the agenda. With Christ at the wheel and the Holy Spirit filling your sails, you can have no excuse for anything other than a blessed life.

Reflections on a Windshield

It was out of context, and it bothered me. Miles away from any sign of civilization, it was the last thing I expected to see as I made my way toward an obscure bend in the Congaree River, my goal for the day.

It was early spring, and I had been hiking for several hours through the Congaree National Park, the last two with no discernible trail under foot. I was relying upon my Magellan Explorist 610 to guide me to a particular spot on the map that had intrigued me. Why the spot interested me I truly don't know, exclusive of the fact that it looked like a place where no human had ever set foot, and I was channeling Marco Polo on this particular morning.

As I made my way through the tangle of vines, roots, and fallen branches that make up the floor of the swamp, my legs were beginning to tire a bit and the bottom of my left foot was reminding me of a childhood encounter with a brown recluse. I must admit it was a relief when I finally broke through the undergrowth to the welcoming sunshine of the river's edge.

It was indeed a beautiful place. The river rolled away around a bend shimmering in the late morning sunshine, a light breeze carried the sweet smell of wisteria my way from somewhere deep in the forest, and the soft sand of the shore was inviting me to have a seat.

I accepted the invitation and reveled for a time in the peace and quiet of the place. The enchanting feeling of being totally separate from the rest of the world enveloped me as I watched a red-tailed hawk come to rest in the high branches of a cypress tree on the opposite shore. The quiet was soon shattered, however, by the raucous cries of a flock of crows as they attempted to dislodge the hawk from his perch. There appeared to be no malice in their efforts, just a way to fight off midday boredom, I suppose. Eventually, though, the hawk tired of their games and took to the air gliding effortlessly down the center of the river toward the aforementioned bend, disappearing into the mist.

As my eyes followed his progress, I noticed a glimmer on the shore—well, actually, back from the shore in the woods about a quarter mile downriver from my location. Bored with resting, I arose and walked through the woods to where I estimated the glimmer originated.

Much to my surprise, I discovered the windscreen from a Model T Ford leaning against a tree. It was a deep brown from decades of weather and rust and hopelessly entangled by years of vine growth, and upon further examination, I noticed the tree itself had grown around the bottom crosspiece, cracking the glass and forever locking the windshield in time and space.

For reasons unknown to me at the time, the presence of that windscreen bothered me. Oh, it was a fascination to me, to be sure, but it had invaded my fanciful idea of being the first to enter this primeval forest. In so doing, it had reminded me that time and space are simply borrowed. It reminded me that we as human beings are living out our lives on a timeline that will eventually end. It left me asking, "I wonder who owned that Ford and if that old windscreen is all that was left behind to indicate he or she walked the planet." I tend to get a little bit morose when my fanciful daydreams are disturbed.

Morose or not, it forced me to ask myself what will be left behind after I depart. In years to come, will some young man happen upon an old silver bullet of a camper—windows broken, tires flat, grown-over with vines, and hidden in the woods for decades—and ask the same question of me?

That question ran laps in my mind as I made my way back to the trailhead that afternoon. What would I leave behind? What legacy would define who I was and/ or am to those who follow? Over and above that, I was forced to ask myself, is my name or my legacy of any importance whatsoever in the scheme of things?

Upon reflection I had to conclude that, no, my legacy is of little importance.

The name of Anthony S. Rowell will be remembered by a pitiful few when I leave this earth. With that understood, I know without a doubt that while my legacy is of little importance, the legacy of Christ and what I can contribute to that legacy is of vast importance. For while my name will be but a fleeting memory to most, the name of Jesus Christ will live forever.

With that in mind I pray my life adds to the legacy of Christ first and foremost, for there can be no greater calling, no greater purpose, and no greater legacy than that. And I pray the same for you.

Tupelo Honey

His beady little eyes looked at me curiously and dared me to move. As he stood on the bank and glared at me, his slathering lips smacked a bit on whatever piece of trash he had picked up. It looked like a piece of old rotten garfish, but I couldn't be sure. I didn't really want to find out, but he was so close and seemed to be enjoying the thing so much I got curious. So I leaned in to get a better look, and then his breath hit me square in the face. Yep, rotten garfish. Once you've smelled it, you never forget it.

It was back in the mid-sixties, and I was sitting in an old plywood fishing boat at Willis Landing. Willis Landing was a nondescript little establishment situated about halfway in-between Port St. Joe and Wewahitchka, Florida, on the banks of the Chipola River. I was waiting on Granny to come back after paying the fare and buying a cricket or two when this hog—not a regular hog, mind you, but a boat landing hog, I think they're bred for the purpose—sauntered up to my boat panhandling. He was pretty adamant about it, too.

It was obvious he didn't plan on leaving my company emptyhanded, but all I had on me that morning was a couple of cans of Vienna sausages, and trust me when I tell you I will fight you, even to this day, if you mess with my Vienna sausages. So he and I were in the proverbial Mexican standoff as we stared at one another. He had the advantage, being a hundred pounds heavier than me, but I was wiry, scrappy, and hungry to boot, which balanced the scales.

I really was in a pickle, though. Other than diving into the river, I had no effective retreat, and having caught all sorts of interesting things out of that river, I had no interest in meeting those critters on their home turf.

As he and I pondered the situation with no solution in sight, the sound of a twelve-gauge cutting loose somewhere in the woods over on the opposite bank drew our attention away from one another for a second or two. But as the sound faded, we went back to our posturing and pondering.

Little did I know the demise of some poor raccoon was to be my salvation. For as the raccoon began his transition from coon to cap, the leftover shot from the blast began to rain down on me and my belligerent companion. For a minute there, the river, my boat, my person, and my beady-eyed visitor were getting peppered pretty good as #8 shot rained down from above.

This happened from time to time at the landing and was more of a nuisance than anything else, but apparently a particularly hot piece of lead landed on a particularly sensitive part of my newfound friend. For as his expression changed from terrifying to terrified, he started screaming like a little girl piglet and headed for cover. Not liking my vulnerable position, I saw my opportunity and sprinted for the bait shed, Granny, and higher ground.

As it turned out, my friend had a family, and as I headed for the shed, his kinfolk began boiling out from underneath the place. Man, he had a lot of mouths to feed, and all those mouths were followed by a sow whose bulk and expression made my erstwhile friend look sweet and cuddly in comparison. Not wanting any of that, I turned back to the river and the relative safety of my boat, but by now my old friend had regained his composure and had outflanked me. I never knew pigs worked in concert, but this crowd had done a fine job of herding me into the woods, where I assumed they were gonna run me down and turn me into bacon.

Now it was my turn to scream like a little girl piglet. As I sprinted toward the woods yelling for Granny, I caught sight of her out of the corner of my eye standing on the bait shed's front porch watching the festivities with an amused expression on her face. I don't know what I expected Granny to do about the situation, but I will admit the smile was a little off-putting.

Laying my hurt feelings aside, I focused on the task at hand and ran as fast as my little bare feet could carry me toward the woods, praying for a tree with a low-hanging branch. Turns out that wasn't needed, because as my entourage and I tore past the bait shed's farthest corner, I heard Granny holler "outhouse"—with a little concern in her voice this time, I might add. It warmed my heart. It warmed my heart and changed my direction, because at her word I noticed off to the left and about ten or fifteen feet past the tree line sat an old greenish-brown outhouse. It could have used a coat of paint or two, and as first choices go, it had a lot to be desired, but any port in a storm as they say. So I dove right in.

There I was trapped in an old outhouse on a hot summer's day surrounded by a bunch of pigs with ill intent in their hearts toward my person. I only thought I was in a pickle before, but now I knew I'd had it for sure. Because on top of everything else, when I dove in and slammed the door, I irritated my newfound hosts, and a low, irate, ominous hum began to vibrate the boards under my bare feet.

As it turns out, the business end of the outhouse was filled to capacity with an odd combination of yellow jackets, honeybees, wasps, and an assortment of multicolored blowflies, as we used to call them. It appeared I had disturbed their midday siesta, and the whole motley crowd was unhappy with me on account of that. So they started this unremitting buzzing. I'll admit that the sound was somewhat alarming, but it was the effect on the atmosphere, intended or otherwise, that was startling.

The air in a Florida swamp in midsummer can be a little thickish sometimes. The air in an outhouse in a Florida swamp in midsummer can be well-nigh solid. The air in an outhouse in a Florida swamp in midsummer with a thousand bees stirring up that air with their angry buzzing can make a young boy yearn for the fragrance of a little rotten garfish.

After weighing my options, I figured I had a better chance of survival with the pigs. So I sighted the front porch through the gaps in the sideboards, and flinging the door open, with head down, I hit the ground running for all I was worth and ran smack into Granny, knocking her down and into the mud. She started laughing on the way down, and I started crying from sheer relief.

It appears my tormentors had grown tired of toying with me. They were all gathered under the porch squealing and grunting and besmirching my good name, I have no doubt.

As I sat in an old rocking chair on the front porch, Granny did something she seldom did. She felt so bad about my exploits that she went to the old store and bought me my own, and I might add my first, little jar of Tupelo Honey, made on the premises. It even had a little label: "Florida's Best Tupelo Honey. Made at Willis Landing, Enjoy!"

Later that night as I sopped up every last bit of honey on the plate with one of Granny's biscuits, it occurred to me just how close the proximity between the outhouse, the pigs, the bees, and the honey was, but it was too late to make any difference. I was already hooked.

The message is simply this: Life can be a mess sometimes, but be patient. God has a plan. Remember that no matter how messy or worrisome things get in your life, He's got this. If God can turn an outhouse, a troublesome hog, an outraged sow, and a thousand angry bees into honey, He can do anything.

For the Birds

I was sitting on my front porch swing the other morning slowly drinking my last cup of coffee. I was doing my best to eke out a little more time for myself to sit and enjoy the beautiful weather before the official day started.

As the coffee cup warmed my palms, I glanced over at the birdfeeders and noticed the wide variety of birds not always seen in South Carolina. It seemed they were on their way north, fleeing the coming heat, and decided to stop off for a bit of breakfast at my house. You see, I have always loved birds, and I try to keep plenty of food on-hand for them should they decide to come by to visit for a spell. If God ever created a glass-half-full creature, it had to be the birds. They start singing at the first sign of light and keep at it all day long until dusk, and then the mockers take the night shift. I suppose the vultures might be an exception, but then again, every rule has to have one.

I counted no less than five different species of birds that morning at my feeders. There was the common house sparrow with an attitude that proves he doesn't consider himself common. A group of them had set up a perimeter around one of the feeders daring anybody to challenge them. I saw a pair of cardinals with the male dressed up in his finest regalia, his mate dressed in her plain house frock following close behind. There were a couple of chickadees tittering about looking for all the world like they were ready for a night on the town with their black hats and ties. The most abundant by far were the cedar waxwings. They look a little sinister with their black masks, but they seem to get along pretty well just the same. An entire flock of them had descended upon the woods that surround my house. This added a bit of bedlam to the peaceful morning. It was a melodious bedlam, though, so I didn't mind. Finally, there was a small group of yellow finches, their bright yellow bodies set off against their black and white wings.

It was truly a smorgasbord of sight and sound and a pleasure to observe. As I watched the interplay between the various species and the individuals themselves,

I was surprised to note that for the most part they got along pretty well. They all wanted the same thing. They wanted a tasty sunflower seed and a quiet place to enjoy it. They wanted to fill their bellies so they could be on their way.

As I watched, I noticed even the sparrows would yield a little space if needed for a waxwing or two to grab a seed and go. I also noticed some of the older birds would not only yield their perches but would actually give seeds to the younger birds around them. At first I simply thought these were the adults feeding their chicks until I remembered that it was February, and nesting was at least a month down the road. Then, to my surprise, I watched as a cedar waxwing gently gave a seed to a yellow finch on the perch beneath. Perhaps the bird was confused by the chaos all around, but it was truly wonderful to see nonetheless, and it got me to thinking. If birds can do it, why can't we?

As I observed all of these birds of various species work out their differences in such a way that all were fed and strengthened for the journey ahead, I was left to wonder why is it that the Body of Christ can't seem to do the same?

With a dark world in desperate need of the light of Christ right outside the door, those of us within spend far too much of our time trying to decide which brand of match and what color candle should be used. And while thanks be to God the world is ignorant of most of this, it is still left hungering for the "fruit of the spirit." The world is still starving for the love that Christ, and Christ alone, offers.

While we within the church may be waxwings, cardinals, and chickadees, we all rest under the comforting wings of Jesus Christ, and we need to remember our differences pale in comparison to the desperate need waiting right outside our door.

Our love for Christ and one another is what nourishes us as we prepare for the journey ahead. It is what strengthens us for the task before us. It is what empowers us to overlook our differences as we focus on the cross of Christ and the sacrifice and love that cross represents.

We all have a job to do, and we must let nothing stand in our way, not even ourselves, for "the harvest is great and the workers are few" (Luke 10:2 NLT).

Rest in the Lord

It was several years ago, as I recall. I had gone to the gym in the futile attempt of tightening what had loosened, and after doing my bit, I was sitting in the sauna. As the heat loosened my muscles, so the peace loosened my mind, and my mind, being freed, burst forth in verse. The subject, however, was a bit odd.

You see, a few weeks before this as I was hiking through the Congaree Swamp, I'd glanced down at the ground. To my surprise and delight there was a dung beetle right smack dab in the middle of the trail. Apparently he had been very industrious, for he had a nice prize rolling in front of him—or in back of him, as the case may be. Where he got the thing I don't know or care to know, but he was sure proud of it nonetheless.

As I was sitting there in the sauna with my mind's eye revisiting the scene, it occurred to me that in all of literature there was probably no verse dedicated to the humble dung beetle. So I wrote a poem in honor of the beetle and his humble task:

Ode to the Humble Dung Beetle

Have you ever heard a dung beetle sing,
midst cow pie and dew on the feld?
There's a gleam in his eye,
as with droppings he plies his trade
for which breath must be held.

As backward he goes
he carries a load of burdens
that few can conceive.
But he's filled with glee
for he knows that we

need him to clean up what we leave.

So next time you see a dung beetle be,
filled with joy and leap high in the air.
For under your feet
he sweepeth the street,
for thus has the Lord placed him there.

Now the question that may well be popping into your mind right now is: "Why in the world is he writing about a dung beetle?" The answer is simple. I am not writing about the dung beetle, per se. I am writing about the joy and contentment felt when a creature knows without doubt that he or she is doing the task for which they were created.

Why the poor dung beetle—poor in my estimation, at least—has been relegated to such a repugnant task is not for he or me to question. He has been given the tools of the trade and a desire to do the best he can in the service of his Creator. In doing his job well, he brings joy to his Creator, and he sleeps the peaceful sleep of the righteous.

He never questions. He never laments his position. He never blames God for his station in life. He simply revels in his service and carries on day in and day out.

How often do we lament the station in which we have been placed? How often do we spend our days dreaming of things to come only to lose the things that are? To quote a great songwriter (who also just so happened to be a Beatle), John Lennon once wrote that "life is what happens to you while you're busy making other plans."

We, as human beings, have been given the great gift of reason and critical thought. We have been blessed with the gift and curse of realizing our mortality. We carry within us the double-edged sword of ambition, which takes us to heights unimagined yet steals our contentment if left unchecked. We find it hard to rest in the Lord, for we are a restless breed.

Life is a balancing act for us all. Most of us hover somewhere between ambition and contentment, laziness and hyperactivity. Finding balance in this life is difficult, to say the least. But amidst the turmoil of life, deep peace and contentment of spirit is available in the person of Jesus Christ.

For whatever our station and whatever our dreams, if Christ is kept foremost in our hearts and minds, and if His will is truly sought throughout our brief earthly existence, then peace and joy will be the bed upon which our lives rest. Then life will no longer be a burden to bear but a joy to experience as we live in the light of His love and rest in the peace of His presence.

Outstreached Arms (Boone Plantation Oak), by Tony Rowell

Happy Now?

Back when I was a boy, I loved to go fishing with my grandparents down in the panhandle of Florida. They are long since gone now, but the memories, the love, and the lessons remain deep in my heart.

I have told you about them before. Granny and Grandpa Tharpe were the perfect grandparents for a little boy. Grandpa was a milkman. He was manly as manly could be, strong as an ox, weather-beaten and the second-best fisherman to ever grace the planet. He was second only to his bride, a fisherwoman by the name of Margaret Jane Jenkins Tharpe, Maggie to those who knew her. That woman could catch a fish in a dry riverbed.

When asked about it, she would simply say the secret was in how you held your tongue and whether or not you chewed your bait long enough before putting it on the hook. Whatever her secret was, it worked. Nobody could out-fish her.

Now Granny was just about as tough and weather-beaten as Grandpa. She had a lot of Creek and Cherokee in her, which made her tough and dark, and those Native-born roots of hers seemed to give her a unique way of teaching lessons to her grandson.

From time to time the old peach tree switch was used, but for the most part she simply said what needed to be said, and that was that. But trust me—once she taught a lesson you had better get it. Once was it. After that, you paid a price for forgetting. I learned very quickly under her tutelage.

For the most part, the lessons she taught me have been retained by me and have held me in good stead over the years. There is one lesson she taught that tends to be a bit troubling, however, because for the life of me, if I'm not careful, I will forget it—and just as she predicted, I will pay the price of a heavy spirit.

One day while Granny and Grandpa and my brother, Mike, and I were down on the Chipola River at my favorite fishing spot, Whiskey Slough, I learned that lesson.

It was one of those lazy summer days when the heat turns your thoughts to shade trees and the humming of the dragonflies invite a nap. My brother, Mike, was in a boat with Grandpa, and I was in another one with Granny. We rented the old wooden jon boats from a fella at Willis Landing, just up the river. They came complete with paddles, leaks, and bailing buckets. Actually, the owner just provided an odd assortment of coffee cans for bailing, while the courage to venture out was provided by the customer.

Well, as the day progressed, everyone was catching fish: bream, shellcracker and the occasional channel cat. Everyone was catching fish but me, that is.

I was about six years of age or so, and the injustice of the whole thing just got the best of me, so I was fussing and fuming and giving my Granny no rest. Of course, that didn't move her from her spot. She was catching fish, and I was not about to be allowed to horn in on the deal. Fishing etiquette cannot be sacrificed, family member or no family member.

As the day lengthened, I caught a fish or two. Actually, it was more than that, but far less than anybody else, and I just wouldn't let up. I griped about Mike catching more than me. I griped about Grandpa catching more than me, and I griped about my boatmate's lack of caring or concern for her poor, disheveled, disconsolate grandson onto whom fate had placed such a heavy burden.

It was somewhere in the midst of one of my more colorful diatribes when Granny decided it was time to teach me a lesson. As I marched on with my litany of injustices, Granny reached down and untied my stringer from the gunnel. After that, she took what few fish I had caught, slowly and methodically removed them from the stringer, and dropped them over the side of the boat back into the coffee-colored water of Whiskey Slough, all the while humming some unrecognizable but very pleasant tune.

In so doing she managed to shut me up. Actually, I was speechless. How could she have done this? Had she lost all reason? It was during this lull in my verbal pity party that Granny looked over at her poor, astonished grandson and said: "Are you happy now? Your stringer isn't half-empty anymore."

Looking back, Granny did me a favor of grand proportions that day. Please note it took me a while to appreciate it, but she taught me that being happy with what you have is a lot better than lamenting over what you don't have. In other words, rejoicing over a stringer that is half-full is much better than crying over a stringer that is half-empty—or as was true in this case, empty altogether.

No Need to Panic

It has been many years since I have had the pleasure of sitting in a jon boat with my Grandpa Tharpe. Most of my memories of those times have faded to black and white over the years, and many have faded further still and drifted off into nostalgia. Once in a while, though, a scene comes back to me as if it were yesterday, in blazing color, with all the sights and sounds intact.

One of those times came back to me a few weeks ago while I was fishing. I was fishing for bass, making artful casts under logs and into the nooks and crannies where the bass tend to hide, when I made an absolutely beautiful cast directly into a hornet's nest. It was a bit of a scramble for a while there, but I got out more or less unscathed, a sting or two under my vest, but that was about it.

Once I regained my normal breathing pattern, my mind went back to a time when I was with Grandpa sitting in a jon boat on the Chipola River down near Apalachicola, Florida. We had just passed by some honeybee hives on the bank, and Grandpa was explaining to me that such bees were gentle and easy to handle, when all of a sudden, my normally taciturn Grandpa started screaming like a little girl and violently boxing his own ears.

It turned out one of those peaceful bees Grandpa so admired had taken offense at the close proximity of our boat to her hive and divebombed right behind my Grandpa's right ear. In so doing she, the bee, got stuck behind the ear piece of my Grandpa's glasses and proceeded to take advantage of the secure place she had found to begin flailing away at my Grandpa with her stinger.

To say I was surprised would be a colossal understatement. My Grandpa never moved very quickly. He was well known for pacing himself, and yet here he was beating himself up with the speed and agility of Muhammad Ali right before my eyes.

My Granny, on the other hand, was on the back seat doing her best to keep from falling out of the boat as laughter completely consumed her. In between gasps she kept yelling at Grandpa to take off his glasses, as she could see the bee, but Grandpa was in full panic mode and never heard a word she said.

Eventually, in a shower of pieces, parts, and lenses, the glasses did come off. The bee was released to fight another day, and calmness descended once again upon the floodplain.

Grandpa looked around sheepishly, gingerly exploring behind his ear with his fingers to assess the damage. Granny was desperately trying to keep a straight face and losing the battle miserably, and I was simply speechless.

I tell this story not because of any deep theological meaning. I tell it mainly because it makes me laugh and allows me to feel young again, at least for a short time.

But there is a lesson to be learned in all of this. Life is unpredictable. One minute you're peacefully floating down the river, and the next thing you know your ear is on fire and you don't know why. When that happens, we are all faced with a choice. We can panic, beat ourselves silly, and accomplish nothing, or we can give it over to God.

In the world in which we live, with wars, terrorism, hunger, financial malaise, and the like, it is very easy to lose sight of our Savior and panic. It is very easy to succumb to the "Chicken Little" mentality and run around screaming as if we have no God at all. But what kind of witness is that? A poor one, I dare say.

We have a God who is greater than anything in the universe. He is greater than Wall Street, greater than terrorists, greater than our theological differences, greater even than our sins.

We have a God who yearns to surround us with His love and power. He longs to protect us. All we need to do is turn to Him.

He is waiting. No need to panic.

A Sow's Song

"Vibraphone, that's it. I've been racking my brain trying to remember the name of that thing. Now who was it that played the fire out of it? Old dude, couple of generations back old, Frank Sinatra old. Goodman? Armstrong? No, maybe it was Rich? No, that's not him, Buddy kept the rhythm. Rich, Richie, Lionel Richie, noooo, that's way wrong, too young and way too syrupy; but the Lionel is on track. Lionel, Lionel, hotel, Lionel, hotel, Lionel, Fairfield Inn Hotel, no, Hampton Inn. Lionel Hampton—got it."

I don't know, but I may have been a little dehydrated when I came across that sow. She was lying on her side happy as the proverbial pig in slop with no less than twelve squirming piglets vying for position. It was breakfast time in Brisas del Mar, and something about that gross of porcine posteriors all lined up in a row reminded me of the vibes and sent my sleep-deprived, dried-up brain off the rails for a bit. The above interior conversation was the result of that derailment.

It was a mighty pretty scene, though, in an organic sort of way. All those little pink piggies bellied up to the bar with their momma singing her low throaty song of love and contentment. Maybe it was the song that reminded me of the vibes and Hampton.

I seem to recall Hampton couldn't contain a slightly offkey growl of sorts as he played the instrument he was created to play. His joy at being right where he was supposed to be, doing what he was made to do, just could not be contained. It had to come out some way, and I think the growl, just like the sow's song, was an unbridled prayer of joy and thanksgiving at having discovered his purpose in this life.

I understood that, and tearing myself away from the scene, I found myself whistling in the early morning mist as I headed back for breakfast with my team. I felt refreshed and new and ready to take on anything.

You see, about a week or so before my piggy epiphany, I'd stepped out of the hustle and bustle of everyday twenty-first-century life and into the pages of a National

Geographic magazine. We were working in Brisas del Mar, a little village eighty or so kilometers south and a century or two away from Cartagena, Colombia.

Brisas del Mar is a little piece of heaven, even if it is hot enough to give Satan pause. Mud homes with thatched roofs line the pitted dirt roads. Laughing children, and gracious how many there are, crowd the doorways and sheepishly wave or hide behind their mother's skirts in faux shyness. At dusk the air is filled with the sounds of laughter and the aroma of a hundred cooking pots with a hundred culinary delights therein, and beneath it all the burros and roosters hold sway with their supporting chorus.

It is the peace of the place, however, as well as many others like it I been blessed to visit over the years, that brings a certain yearning to my soul. For that peace is not to be found in the glorious cacophony of sight, sound, and smell, but it is to be found in my heart and in my soul.

For me, at least in my life, the peace of Christ, the promised rest of the Creator, is found in working with my brothers and sisters, wherever they may be, for the Kingdom of God in a hands-on, dirt-way-up-under-your-fingernails sort of way.

My prayer for you is that you find that place of peace and of rest in your life, wherever it may be. But never forget it takes courage, faith, and fortitude. For you must seek to find.

Remember the promise? "Ask and it will be given to you; seek and you will find; knock and the door will be opened to you. For everyone who asks receives; he who seeks finds; and to him who knocks, the door will be opened" (Matthew 7:7-8 NIV).

Spring Steel

I have a short list of folks with whom I wouldn't want to tangle if my life depended on it. There are only four individuals on the list, and surprisingly enough, they are all of the female persuasion. That being said, in all four cases, given the occasion of a confrontation, I would scream like a little girl, tuck my tail between my legs, and head for the hills running like a scalded dog. I would go further in my description, but I'm running short on clichés. Suffice it to say, I wouldn't mess with any of them, and I would advise you to do the same.

In no particular order these esteemed ladies are my momma, Bobbie Jean Tharpe Rowell; her momma, Margaret Jane Jenkins Tharpe, better known as Granny; Granny's neighbor to the left, Miss Irene (Irene stands alone in needing no further designation; Irene is just Irene); and my Great Aunt Doshey on my Grandpa Tharpe's side.

My momma was a 95-pound combination of angel food cake, devil's food cake, sweet buttermilk, and Texas Pete. She was the consummate Southern lady with excellent manners, beautiful features, a soft lilting voice, the memory of a pachyderm, and a spine of tempered steel. My mom was a beautiful red rose nestled among thorns, where the fragrance was intoxicating and the thorns had barbs. To love and be loved by Bobbie Jean Rowell was a gift from above, but you messed with my mother at your own peril.

My Granny was the woman who bore and raised my mom. It seems to me that should be all the description needed. Granny passed down her strength, determination, and self-reliance to Mom. Mom added a bit of spice and a pleasant refinement to the mix, but given the need to stand firm, the granite that was my Granny would shine through as the flint and steel that was my mom. I've said before God gave me a jewel when he gave me my Granny, but that jewel had a sharp edge or two that were best avoided.

Miss Irene, Granny's next-door neighbor, was a sight for terrified eyes. She topped out at around five feet tall, I figure, and trapped inside those five feet were two hundred pounds of spring steel, rawhide, and gristle. Covering her frame was a dirty gray house frock she wore day in and day out without exception. Apparently, she didn't believe in washing her hair all too often, either. She figured it would mess with her mystique, I suppose.

I'm not one to dream very much, but should Miss Irene venture into my subconscious, I'd wake up in a cold sweat every time. That being said, on the late July afternoon when that hot grease on my Granny's stove caught fire and burned down the kitchen, Miss Irene was the first one on the scene to help as best she could.

She hugged my Granny, helped her hide the tears, and took a terrified eight-year-old off Granny's hands and fed him a fine meal, as I recall. Then she stood solid and firm as a dear friend and fine neighbor to my Granny. You really don't know a person until you live through a crisis with them.

I will always describe my Great Aunt Doshey as a high-haired woman of the Old South. That woman had a jet-black beehive hairdo until the day she died. I believe they had to extend her coffin a bit to accommodate the thing. Aunt Doshey stood five-feet-nothing while standing on a three-foot ladder, but with that beehive hairdo of hers, she could try out for the Harlem Globetrotters.

Aunt Doshey was a charter member of the local Pentecostal church, so according to her, she could never tell a lie. Nonetheless, she swore up and down she never used hair color, despite the fact that her eyebrows were as gray as General Lee's uniform, while that smokestack of a hairdo was always black as soot.

Despite that trivial moral lapse, she did have a couple of redeeming qualities. She had a really nice backyard with good trees for climbing and soft dirt for digging, which was appealing to a young boy. Her most alluring quality in the eyes of a little kid, however, lay in the fact that she was addicted to Coca-Cola. Every now and again, when Granny wasn't watching, she would let me sneak one. You see, Coca-Cola and such frivolities were forbidden on Sunday afternoons according to my Granny's take on the Ten Commandments.

Speaking of the Ten Commandments, Aunt Doshey was a proponent for all of them, as well as the rest of Deuteronomy, Chronicles 1 and 2, and every other last ounce of the Good Book. You see, Aunt Doshey was a dyed-in-the-wool, hard-shell, Bible-believing, slain in the Spirit, washed in the blood, Church of God Pentecostal, and you simply did not want to cross her. You just didn't. She was unwavering in her belief, vocal in her convictions, and swift in her wrath.

Now while I must admit she did scare me a bit as a child, in retrospect I truly appreciate some things about her. I respect and admire her strength of faith in Jesus Christ and His saving grace. I appreciate her fearlessness when doing battle for the Lord, and I also appreciate her total reliance on the Word of God as written in the

King James Version, circa 1611.

Now considering my affinity for the NIV, she might have a bit of a problem with me in that area. You see, to her it was King James or nothing. She had been taught and believed that the NIV, ASV, RSV, and any other V other than the KJV were heretical, and that anybody reading them was in imminent danger of the wrath of God descending on them right then and there. After all, if the King James was good enough for Jesus, then it was good enough for everybody. All that aside, I sure wish we had an army of Aunt Dosheys these days.

So let me ask you: Is there an Aunt Doshey hidden deep within? Where do you stand when it comes to the Kingdom of God? Do you have the strength, compassion, and conviction of my memories? I pray that you do, for the world is in desperate need for the Savior you have to offer.

"Therefore, my beloved brethren, be ye stedfast, unmoveable, always abounding in the work of the Lord, forasmuch as ye know that your labour is not in vain in the Lord" (1 Corinthians 15:58 KJV).

Love you, Aunt Doshey!

Outstretched Arms

It was as if they had been reaching for one another forever. Like two young lovers separated by time and space, unable to fulfill their longings, until one day, after years and perhaps decades of yearning, they touch. They intertwine in a loving embrace never to be broken. They sigh in their contentment knowing full well that they will never part, not in this lifetime, at least. As time slowly marches on, their love for one another never fades, but it does change with the years. From intense passion and voracious longing to quiet companionship and stalwart support, their love never becomes cracked and dried. It only cures and strengthens with time until one day, they can tell no longer who is supporting whom. They have become one, equally reliant and equally supportive.

Now with their journey accomplished and the struggle behind them, they can rest. So on their outstretched arms, surrounded by a love full of years, a lone mockingbird fills the night air with his song. The song is eerie in the night. The Lowcountry fog has risen and now filters the sound, adding mystery and just a touch of otherworldliness to the melody. The ever-present Spanish moss shrouds the lovers with a covering of lace, the intimacy of which gives a visitor pause. This is a private, personal world, and to enter in seems almost profane. But with the dawn come the admirers and the dreamers of days past and the evidence of God's blessing on these magnificent creatures.

The golden light of dawn comes with the morning, and with the light, the majesty of these venerable old trees is made evident. As the sunlight filters through the age-old branches and dapples the fallen leaves beneath, a sense of timeless peace fills the space. As the morning mists dance within the light, the foreboding of last night vanishes to be replaced by a welcoming, ageless calm. But it is in the storm where the true majesty of these old souls comes to the fore. As the lightning flashes above and the earth shakes to the sound of thunder beneath, these old trees remain at their post—never faltering, never cowering, forever challenging Mother Nature to do her worst while they do their best. Shaking their fists at the sky and standing their ground defiant, undefeated and unashamed.

For 270-some-odd years, these same trees have stood sentry over the land. They have seen the birth of a nation. They have witnessed beneath their outstretched limbs the tragedy of that same nation at war with itself. They have felt the pain of brother against brother, of families torn asunder, and have looked on in horror as human beings were bought and sold like cattle.

They have listened to the melody of children, slave and free, black and white, playing beneath their sheltering limbs. They have heard the old men talk of times gone by and the young men speak of the future. They have reveled at the sound of hymns being sung and prayers being raised to their God. They have seen love and hate, joy and heartbreak, sorrow and rejoicing. They have seen it all.

I wonder what they think of us. In the course of eleven generations, they have seen much: wars and rumors of wars, nations rising against nations, kingdoms against kingdoms.

Do they think us evil or good, a blessing or a curse? Does the good outweigh the bad? Does the holy outweigh the evil? I pray it does, but to be honest, there have been times when I have wondered.

There have been times when the evil in the world has pressed down on my soul; times when the darkness appears so pervasive that I fear there is no escaping; times when Satan appears for all the world to have won the day.

Then I am reminded of a young man, a man of peace and love, a man filled to overflowing with understanding and compassion, and I remember a world dead-set against Him. I remember Him bloody, battered and bruised for my sake standing His ground defiant, undefeated, and unashamed. From the very cross He shakes His fist in Satan's face declaring, "You do your worst; I will do my best."

I remember my Lord and Savior Jesus Christ rising up on Easter morning declaring "There is a better way; love trumps all!"

Then it comes to my mind that I am His child, and I know then that no matter how much the darkness threatens, the light will always win the day. No matter the storm, with Christ comes peace.

Check Your Seams

Many years ago, I was driving down an old dirt road in Lexington County when I noticed what appeared to be the nose of an old Carolina jon boat winking at me from underneath a tattered tarpaulin behind a dilapidated outbuilding. So I pulled to the side of the road to take a closer look. Afraid somebody would call the cops if I lingered too long, I made a quick assessment of the boat's nose and its tail, which was sticking out of the other end of the tarp, and headed on down the road.

From what I saw, the paint was all but gone, the transom was rotten, the bottom had some suspicious cracks in it, the seats were mildewed to within an inch of their lives, and from the evidence at hand, it appeared a large bird had been nesting in the tree above it. Basically, the thing was a lost cause. Nonetheless, being the eternal optimist, I decided then and there that if I could figure out a way to sell the idea to Mary without an excessive amount of shuckin' and jivin', I wanted that thing.

As many of you know, in my previous life I was a cabinetmaker, and I just knew that if I were to gain that boat, I could make it into something. I had dreams of restoring that neglected old boat, once again making it the fine watercraft I knew it to be.

To my surprise, Mary didn't object too much. She figured it would keep me out of the house, I suppose. So the next day, I went back and knocked on the door like I owned the place, and when an elderly gentleman came to the door, I made him an offer he could have easily refused, but didn't. For the sum of fifty bucks and a smile, I brought home my prize.

Well, that fifty bucks grew as I began the work, but it was worth it. I turned that fourteen-foot disaster area into a thirteen-foot beauty. She sported a new transom, new seats, beautifully restored woodwork, and a nice paint job. The bottom was repaired and strengthened with fiberglass. A depth finder, compass, and other neat gadgets were installed, and the icing on the cake was a brand new Mercury 9.9 outboard motor perched on the new transom.

I stepped back when it was finished and knew my Grandpa Tharpe would be proud. His imagined pride soon worked its way into my chest, which puffed out a bit, and head, which grew a bit, and for a while there, I was a mess.

Finally, the day came when I was to take the boat, now christened the "Margaret Jane" after my Granny Tharpe, up to the river to try her out. I headed up to the Little River Landing just past the traffic circle in Saluda County. As I drove in, I noticed heads turned as she passed by, and I was fit to be tied. I was ready to bust, as my Granny would say. You would have thought that boat was the head cheerleader, homecoming queen, and valedictorian combined, I was so proud.

So I strutted in, paid my two dollars, and made sure the seats were set right, the trolling motor was secure, the battery was hot, and the Pepsis were cold. I backed her in, and she sure was a sight. As she came off of the trailer, she sat high in the water as pretty as you please for about thirty seconds.

And then, with the sun glinting off of her bow, she went down like a lead weight.

To my dismay, I watched as she quietly settled down into the water. Time tends to slow down at moments like that. Your blood turns to molasses in your veins, your feet become lead, your mind struggles to take it in, and you just stand there stunned. My stupor was short-lived, though, for with a muffled thump, a slight grating sound, and a satisfied gurgle or two, she settled to the bottom and came to rest.

When the buzzing in my ears subsided, I noticed sounds behind me, and as I turned around, I discovered I had an audience. Five or six fellow fishermen were behind me watching the travesty unfold with what appeared to be expressions of detached curiosity on their faces. When they noticed I had noticed them, however, they—being fishermen and boat lovers themselves—sprang into action, and within a few minutes my soggy masterpiece was back on the trailer.

As the water cascaded out of the drain I had so carefully drilled in the bottom of the transom, a fisherman by the name of Jimmy held up the drain plug and, with a pleasant smile, informed me that in the future it would be best to plug the drain before I launched the boat. I thanked him and, muttering under my breath, headed home.

It has been about fifteen years since that incident, but every now and again I run into Jimmy, and his sly grin reminds me that pride does indeed come before a fall.

I tell this story to make a simple point. Namely, it doesn't matter how pretty your boat is or how proud you are of it, if there is a hole in the bottom and you don't plug the hole, trouble will soon follow.

The same holds true for your spiritual life. So check your seams. Is your spirit leaking out and letting the world in to invade your peace and tarnish your joy? If so, then shore that leaking life up with prayer and study and doing the things of God.

Life is way too short to spend it sitting on the bottom looking up.

For Want of Bread

I am writing this as a man in my fifties with a bad back, a broken ACL in my left knee, high cholesterol, questionable teeth, no prostate because of cancer, a little hearing loss in my left ear, a left foot that goes from good to bad in a millisecond due to an encounter with a brown recluse spider, and an inability to remember where I left my reading glasses the last time I put them down, with the matching inability to see them once I find them.

Other than that, I am a virile, strong-willed man in great shape, for the shape I'm in, with a God who loves me, a wife who loves me, and children and grandchildren who love me. I don't believe I could have written a better life for myself had I tried, and yet from time to time I worry. I fret. I lament—not for myself, mind you, but for others.

You see, I have three beautiful grandchildren with three more on the way, and I worry for them. The world we live in is treacherous, but not in the way you might think. Yes, there are the physical dangers: the wars, the crime, the disease, and all. There are drugs and alcohol and all sorts of other things that tempt and destroy the young and old alike. Over and above that, there are the sins we love to engage in, forgetting that with the sin come the wages, and the bill never fails to come due.

Life is filled with wondrous things to be enjoyed and treasured to be sure, but there are also the back alleys and the blind curves of life, and without instruction and guidance, those who follow in our footsteps walk on shaky ground.

Mary and I went on vacation for a week of camping in the Upstate of South Carolina recently. On the way home, we passed through a wonderfully quaint little town. In its heyday during the gold rush many years ago, Mount Carmel, South Carolina, must have been a blushing beauty.

Now, though, as quaint as she still remains, the blush is gone. The ravages of age—and the neglect of a generation or two of folks focused more upon their present comforts as opposed to the heritage of the past and the strength therein—have left the little town bereft of life save for a few stalwart families.

Beautiful antebellum homes, many on the historical register, lay deserted, neglected, and falling in upon themselves. The old town hall leans a bit as if tired from the strain, but saddest of all are the two churches. Those beautiful buildings, places where in years gone by believers rejoiced to hear the word of God preached, now lay boarded up and hollow.

We often hear of famine in Africa or some other far-off place, and we cry at the thought that the children go to bed hungry. We often look with disgust and rage at the reports of food stockpiled and rotting while the adults use it as leverage in their attempt to gain power or wealth or some other temporal thing. We don't understand how anyone could let a child starve for want of bread when bread is available.

When I look out over the landscape of our country, I wonder just how many children are starving for want of the "Bread of Life." As we stockpile doctrine upon tradition, tradition upon theology, theology upon denomination, denomination upon liberal, liberal upon conservative, my way upon your way, and your way upon mine, I fear we are in danger of losing our way. For we are called to follow "The Way," our Lord and Savior Jesus Christ, and Him alone.

We cannot let anything stand in the way of the Gospel of Jesus Christ and the saving grace that message carries. We must never allow anything to prevent the Bread of Life from reaching the children that follow in our footsteps.

Whatever differences we as a people may have pale when compared to the joy, the love, the peace, and the blessed unity offered through a relationship with Christ Jesus.

The children are counting on us! Dear Lord, please help us not to fail.

Shootin' Snakes

I was seven or eight years old at the time, and goodness gracious, it was hot as blazes that day. Shoot, it was so warm on the Florida Panhandle that Wednesday afternoon that Satan himself sought the shade of a cypress and a tall glass of sweet iced tea. The world wavered under the heat, but if you squinted just so and held your cap at just the right angle to block the sun, you could see the far-off forms of two little boys through the heaving air, one with an old Zebco 33 in his hands and one with a single-shot .22 caliber rifle resting comfortably on his shoulder. They were standing at the far end of the Dead Lakes Dam wondering what to do next.

I held the Zebco and my companion, Roy, had hold of the .22, and at the time we were debating the best way to shoot a snake. I voted for a shotgun at a considerable distance, but Roy said the old .22 was best at any distance—provided, of course, you knew what to do with it. It was that last little jab that raised the hackles on the back of my neck. Eight years old or not, I considered myself a darn good shot and pretty close to fearless on top of that, and such a statement challenged both assumptions.

The catalyst for this conversation was swimming seventy or eighty feet, give or take a few, off to the left of us out in a little lagoon of sorts. The water was flat and mirrored in the midday lull, so it was easy to make out the markings of the moccasin as he thrashed in the water desperately trying to escape. He looked to be somewhere around three or four feet long, a little chubby on account of the ample food supply and more than a little upset with his current situation. He had recently made a decision that had not gone his way.

You see, Roy and I had been fishing together all morning, and by the time noon came around, we were growing a little restless and looking for some mischief to get into. Roy's dad, whose name I can't recall, owned the little rundown motel, bait shop, and pool hall located a quarter mile or so from the far end of the dam. We were headed that way in search of opportunity when Roy noticed this moccasin swimming away from the bank.

Now I was proud of my casting ability and Roy knew it, so it didn't take much prodding to get me to see if I could hit that moving snake with the rubber worm on the end of my line.

If I say so myself, I did pretty good. I dropped that lure right on the top of that snake's head while he was moving at a pretty good clip. As it turns out the snake took offense at this, whipped around, sunk his fangs into my rubber worm, got one of his fangs caught in the weed guard of my number 2 Eagle Claw weedless hook, and was stuck fast.

The initial debate was between cutting the line and shooting the snake, but Roy would have none of that. So without another word, he ran down to his house to get the rifle. When he came back with the .22, I was a little dubious. I mean having an angry, offended moccasin on the line is bad enough, but having an injured, angry, offended moccasin on the line raises things to a brand-new level.

All of that considered, the debate ended and the competition began when Roy uttered those now infamous words, "… provided, of course, you knew what to do with it."

Since I had the Zebco and Roy owned the rifle, he got the first shot, and up until that moment I truly thought I could shoot. As he raised the rifle to his shoulder, he was transformed. He was no longer a skinny little boy with an oversized rifle in his hands. The two became one as with a single fluid motion he raised the rifle, sighted his target, and relieved the tension on my line.

I was truly impressed—more so, I might add, than Roy's momma. She came running at the report of the rifle, fully intent upon tanning our hides for scaring her to death. That being said, even she had to give begrudging respect to her son for a shot that left me with nothing more than a rubber worm, a couple of fangs, and a brand-new appreciation for Roy.

As I finish this story, I am looking for a moral in it. When I lay down to go to

Dead Lakes, by Tony Rowell

sleep last night, I was wondering what to write, and this old story came to mind. When I awoke, it remained lodged there, so I figure Christ wants it told.

I will leave it to you to discover what He wants you to get out of it, but I can tell you this: I will think twice before I go to picking on a moccasin again. The next time there might not be a Roy around to bail me out.

"When tempted, no one should say, 'God is tempting me.' For God cannot be tempted by evil, nor does he tempt anyone; but each person is tempted when they are dragged away by their own evil desire and enticed. Then, after desire has conceived, it gives birth to sin; and sin, when it is full-grown, gives birth to death" (James 1:13-15 NIV).

"Be alert and of sober mind. Your enemy the devil prowls around like a roaring lion looking for someone to devour" (1 Peter 5:8 NIV).

La Biblia, by Tony Rowell

Keep On Hangin' On!

The day my Granny lost the tip of her finger is one that will forever stand out in my memory. She didn't lose the whole thing, mind you, but just enough to remind her to be more careful in the future.

As so many of my memories begin, I was down in the panhandle of Florida on the Chipola River fishing with Granny and Grandpa Tharpe. It was a Wednesday, and everything was just perfect. The sky was just the right shade of blue, with beautiful white puffy clouds running across it—you know, those clouds that make you see things like Mickey Mouse or Abe Lincoln in them. The water lapped gently against the side of the old rented jon boat we sat in, and the shade was more inviting than usual. It was so inviting, in fact, that we had accepted the invitation.

We were sitting under the arches of an old cypress tree with our cane poles fanned out in every direction, waiting for the bream and shellcracker to come to their senses and have a taste.

The first thing to hit the line that morning hit on what my Granny called her taut line. That is a line coming off of a rod and reel with a Number Ten hook on the end. Above that were two slip leads sitting on top of a split shot and no cork.

She always had her taut line set out on the off chance that a big channel cat would succumb to its charms. She usually put a big worm or a piece of liver on the hook and let it sit just off the bottom.

Well, on this particular morning, the first thing to take her up on her offer was a little bitty snapping turtle. It wasn't one of those cute little green things you find at the pet store, but a miniature alligator snapper. The thing wasn't much bigger than my hand back then, and I was seven or so, so it looked more like a pet than a menace. It was really cute. So Granny was not paying as much attention as she should have, and when she was just about ready to toss the thing back into the deep, it turned and, with an offended air, clamped down on to my granny's left middle finger and refused to let go.

I have written before of the time when my Granny washed my brother's mouth out with soap for daring to say the word "darn" in casual conversation, so it was a shock to me to find out just what she thought about that little creature's family. I will never forget the tongue-lashing that little thing received—and I will also never forget the sound of Grandpa's laughter as Granny did everything but jump in the river to relieve herself of the burden that had so recently been placed upon her. But it did not matter one lick. The little turtle hung on with such tenacity that nothing, and I mean nothing, my Granny tried would dislodge him.

After a time, though, he was rewarded for his effort when with a slight clicking sound his little jaws met one another, and he returned home with a smug smile and a tasty morsel of one of the greatest grannies to ever grace the planet. Granny, now being relieved of her burden, dipped her finger in the river to clean it, wrapped it up, and joined Grandpa in his laughing—and then got back down to fishing.

I once read that the Christian's greatest fear is not that he or she will be damned to hell, but rather that Christ will be overrun. In other words, we worry that from the evidence at hand, the things that Christ stands for—the love, the justice, the peace—will be overwhelmed and defeated by the powers set up against such things. It is at times such as these that we are called to display spiritual tenacity. We are called to wait upon the Lord.

We are to hold on to the last breath in the knowledge that our God is God and can never be overcome no matter how things appear.

The hardest thing for you and me to do sometimes is to wait upon the Lord, but that is exactly what we are called to do. We are called to tenaciously wait upon the Lord, but waiting is not enough. We must also be tenacious in our work for the Lord while we wait upon Him.

No matter what forces are arrayed against us, we must resist the evil, resist the hatred, and resist the pain this world tends to traffic in, and bring goodness, love, and healing to bear against those who would destroy us. Once again that takes tenacity—endurance fortified with the faith that God cannot be defeated.

I challenge each of us to be people of tenacious faith. No matter what the world is doing, believe. No matter how bad it looks, believe. No matter what you are going through, believe.

We must faithfully trust that our God is God and work with Him to overcome all obstacles, whether spiritual or practical, to further His Kingdom in heaven and on earth.

So be a spiritual snapper. Trust that God Almighty is God Almighty. Don't hide. Don't give up. Don't cut and run. Hang on to your faith no matter what the circumstance may say. Hang on and work for the Kingdom. Give it all you have. Give Christ all you have. Never, never let go! Never ever give up!

No matter what, believe that our God is God and that Christ, and Christ alone, will see us through the fires of this life and bring us unscathed and joyful into the next.

That is what faith is all about.

I'll Be Watching You

She was working her way up toward the ceiling, having a time squeezing herself through whenever she came to a place where the top of the glass panes got too close to the screen. If the old jalousie windows had been closed, she'd have done fine, but it was hot, mid-July, and open they were. The air was still. There was no breeze to be had, even this late in the evening, but having those old porch windows opened offered hope that something would stir and cool me off a bit. I watched her for a while, but then my six-year-old mind drifted to something else. Besides, katydids were a dime a dozen on the panhandle of Florida in mid-July.

I was having trouble falling asleep. I wasn't quite scared; maybe nervous. A little uneasy is the best way to put it, I suppose. You see, this was my first night sleeping solo on Granny's front porch, and when the world got quiet, my imagination came to life.

Before this Mike, my older brother, had been sleeping out there with me. To my mind, at least, the presence of an eight-year-old tended to keep the monsters at bay. But now here I was, six years old, naked, exposed, and more than a little bit concerned for my well-being.

You see, Mike and I had been given the option earlier that evening of either staying at Granny Tharpe's house or heading out to the beach cottage to spend the night with Grandmother Rowell. Now I have always been quick with my words, often to my detriment, but this time my speed came in handy. Before Mike's first word had cleared leather, I called dibs on Granny's house, sending him to the sandspur and palmetto bug capital of northwest Florida: Panama City Beach in the mid-sixties. No harm, no foul, though; Mike has always enjoyed having more sand than mud underfoot, while I have always preferred the contrary, so Grandma and the beach cottage suited him fine.

That left me alone on the front porch with my overactive imagination and the aforementioned katydid. For the record, it is startling just how loud one of those critters can be in close proximity, but that has no bearing on this story in that my katydid was concentrating on her climbing and kept her own counsel.

As a town settles in for the night and all goes soft and quiet, it is curious how the smallest of sounds can travel distances unimagined during the day. As the darkness deepens and the silence grows, an eerie echo ripens and somehow attaches itself to those previously insignificant sounds. That unearthly echo gives the sounds power, and heady with their newfound authority, they can reach deep into a young boy's psyche to produce unimagined terrors.

A beagle's noontime bark becomes the yowling of a dozen hellhounds deep in the night. The wail of a policeman's siren becomes the screech of a newly released spirit fresh from the grave. Before long, a young mind given free rein is peopled with apparitions and phantoms untold.

As I mentioned, though, in spite of my imaginings, I was more uneasy than scared. Even at that early age, my mother's desire to raise independent children was bearing some fruit in my life. So as the unconstrained spirits shrieked and the hellhounds bayed at the moon, the little island that was Tony Rowell drifted off to sleep.

A moment later, I sat bolt upright in bed as a deafening trumpet blast shattered the night air. The heaving light confused my senses, and the quaking under my bed completed the trifecta of terror that seemed to be coming at me from all sides.

It lasted but a second, and I know that as the fire engine continued its frantic way down 17th Street, its heroic tenants were unaware of the traumatized boy they left behind, but traumatized I was. To this day the sound of a siren late in the evening rekindles this memory, threatening the stillness within.

I lay back down, no longer uneasy, but rather terrified and trembling. And it was then that I felt the eyes, those thoughtful eyes, watching me. My grandpa was sitting in an old rocker, cup of coffee in hand, watching over me. I have no idea how long he had been there, but when my eyes met his, he grinned. He never said a word, he just gave a sly smile and nodded.

And while my trembling continued unabated for a time, my fear, my terror, vanished in an instant.

As the years have passed, I have often pondered over this reminiscence of mine. I never asked him, and Grandpa never offered any explanation as to why, in the middle of the night, he sat sipping coffee while watching over his sleeping grandson. In truth, this occurrence, so vivid in my mind, was never mentioned.

Was Grandpa really there, or was my young mind simply seeking comfort in its own imaginings? Was Grandpa really there, or did something mystical and amazing take place?

I have no idea, but this I know. In life there will be struggles. There will be sorrows.

And when things get tough and fear threatens to overtake you, remember the words of the psalmist:

"I lift up my eyes to the hills—where does my help come from? My help comes from the Lord, the Maker of heaven and earth. He will not let your foot slip—he who watches over you will not slumber; indeed, he who watches over Israel will neither slumber nor sleep. The Lord watches over you—the Lord is your shade at your right hand; the sun will not harm you by day, nor the moon by night. The Lord will keep you from all harm—he will watch over your life; the Lord will watch over your coming and going both now and forevermore" (Psalm 121).

La Biblia

He lived in a derelict, old, thatched-roof mud hut. It sat a little ways down from the compound where the team was staying during our brief time in Brisas Del Mar, Colombia, a few years ago.

I had seen him before this particular morning. He would slowly work his way up and down the street from time to time during the day, and the one thing you could not help but notice was the deference everyone in town would show toward him. They would tip their hats and bow their heads. They would always give way, and I even saw a curtsy or two from some of the older ladies late one afternoon. He was greatly loved, but more than that, he was revered. They called him "la Biblia"—the Bible.

I don't know his full name, but Juan is what he had asked me to call him the day before. I had introduced myself that day, hat off of course, as he crossed the street. It appeared to amuse him just a little when upon his asking I gave my name as Antonio. He was gracious and kept his grin at bay, but his eyes chuckled. He couldn't help that.

On that meeting he had asked me how old I was. I told him I was fifty-seven years of age, and he laughed. As he shuffled off, I heard him say "bambino" under his breath with a snicker. As it turns out, The Bible was ninety-nine years of age with a birthday coming a few weeks after our leaving.

The next morning I got up very early, before light. I will admit this is indeed not my custom, but it is difficult to sleep when the air is dead still, the humidity is sitting somewhere around one hundred percent, and the temperature has only cooled down to the mid-nineties overnight. So up I was, like it or not.

I decided that since I was already up and stirring, I would try to catch the sunrise on film. So I grabbed my camera, broke my own rules, and left the compound all alone as the eastern sky was just changing from blackish blue to bluish black. I turned left and headed up the hill to find the best vantage point.

As I was passing by a disheveled hut, I noticed an old tallow candle sitting on a little table just inside the door. The power was off once again, so breakfast was cooking over a small fire out front, while the candle glowed within. Sitting on a milking stool tending the fire was Juan. He looked up, smiled that engaging toothless grin of his, and invited me to join him.

He motioned to the chair just inside the door, and I went to retrieve it. When I looked inside the little house, I saw all of The Bible's earthly possessions in an instant.

Over in the far corner, a woven pallet lay on the dirt floor for sleeping, and scattered elsewhere were a rickety table to hold a plate or two and perhaps a candle, a broken ladder back chair, an odd cooking pot or two, and the milking stool.

We had a nice breakfast together of hoecake. His was almost as good as my Granny's, and his coffee was so stout it needed chewing before you could take a sip.

Sitting there, I could feel the man's contentment with his life. While enjoying the hoecake and coffee, it came to my mind that the boots on my feet cost more than everything this man owned, including his house. Yet I found myself envying him.

He was happy. He was content. He was at total peace with himself and the world around him. The sundry lines on his weather-worn face all pointed upward in a smile. His eyes were milky with age, but they held a deep serenity and a quiet contempt for the world around him. His whole demeanor spoke of peace. Worry was not in his lexicon.

I knew then why those who knew him called him "The Bible." He epitomized the message contained therein.

My Spanish is poor on a good day, and Juan's English was nonexistent; but we managed somehow to communicate pretty well for that hour or so. It was one of those times, those few instances in life, which will remain in my memory as a blessing and a true gift from God.

In parting, I asked him how he had managed to live so long. Ninety-nine is a valiant achievement anywhere, and much more when you consider the conditions under which Juan had spent his life. He didn't answer me right off.

The sun was above the horizon by now. I had missed my photo opportunity, but by God's grace, I had received something much greater.

As the sun continued to rise, the kids started their daily cacophony of sound. The cooks chopped wood for the fires and prepared the morning meals. The men did this and that in preparation for the day. All the while, I was getting antsy wanting to get started on the day's work when Juan looked up at all of it and then at me and grinned.

"Demasiado rápido, más lento," he said. "Too fast, slower."

It is refreshing when you run into a person who has things in perspective, isn't it?

You don't find them very often, but every now and again someone, usually someone older than the hills like Juan, has learned the value of peace and quiet, of rest and contentment, and is willing to share.

To be around such a person is a tonic for the soul.

Philippians 4:4-7, "Rejoice in the Lord always. I will say it again: Rejoice! Let your gentleness be evident to all. The Lord is near. Do not be anxious about anything, but in everything, by prayer and petition, with thanksgiving, present your requests to God. And the peace of God, which transcends all understanding, will guard your hearts and your minds in Christ Jesus."

Colombian Tailgunner, by Tony Rowell

The Bullfight

The upward angle of my memories reminds me of just how young we are when our brains begin to crinkle; when thoughts, feelings, and memories start slipping down into the crooks and crannies; when our consciousness begins filling the crevices of our mind.

I couldn't have been more than three or four, perhaps younger, as I looked up into Grandma Rowell's eyes searching for a hint of weakness, a glimmer of hope that she would relent.

The old house was large, creaky, and cold—fertile ground for a young mind in search of goblins and just the kinda place where a monster could slide under your bed unseen. I had heard one breathing in the night, that soft rasping sound that only a ghoul can make, and fear had gripped me. When the breathing slowed and became rhythmic, I figured he was asleep, so I climbed down as quietly as possible and softly padded my way down the hall to Grandma's room where the lamplight was warm and inviting as it flowed out from beneath the door.

Grandma did not believe in indulging the whims of a child, but the look in my frightened eyes must have touched something within, for her features softened a bit, and she invited me to climb up into the bed with her for a spell.

There is nothing like a feather bed. For those who have never been cradled in the arms of a hundred geese, I have pity. For those who have, then you understand the consolation that simply lying back and allowing the softness to envelop you can bring. For you see while Grandma did not believe in indulging children, she did from time to time pamper herself, and this bed was her pride and joy.

As I settled in and snuggled down, the familiar smell of wisteria came to my nostrils coupled with the ever-present odor of mothballs resting alongside Bengay, added for pungency and zest. Here and ever after, singly or in combination, those odors send me back to that old house, that easy bed, my Grandma Rowell, and a story.

As I sidled up beside my Grandma, she reached over and switched off the lamp.

There was a streetlight somewhere nearby that cast the shadow of magnolia leaves on the wall. As my sleepy eyes watched the shadows dancing on the breeze, Grandma told me the story of the bullfight for the first time.

Grandma had traveled to Mexico as a young girl and returned with a wanderlust that you could hear in her voice and see in her eyes if you looked close enough, but no one ever did. She yearned to see the world, to visit exotic places, and to live life to the fullest, but things happened. Marriage, three children, and life arrived, and after a time, all that remained of her longing was the story of this ancient bullfight, but Lord have mercy, could my Grandma tell a tale. She had a gift for it.

The details have drifted with time, but the images remain. As Grandma painted the story, in my young mind I could hear, I could smell, I could see the crowd working itself into a frenzy. Those pictures painted so long ago remain. As I write this, I see the picadors tormenting the poor creature. Through a haze of dust, I see the angry snorting bull, pawing; the matador proud with his red cape and his exaggerated machismo heaves and swells as the midday heat rises from the ring. Grandma would always pause when she spoke of the matador and sigh. First love, I suppose. His torn body carried from the field would finish her story. Fresh pain rising, Grandma teared up every time she told it.

A strange bedtime story for a frightened child to be sure, but it suited me fine. I awoke the next morning to the sound of rustling magnolia leaves just outside of Grandma's bedroom window with a budding wanderlust newly handed down.

To this day the sound of a distant freight train or the sight of a contrail laid out behind a passing 747 awakens a yearning within me to go.

It is amazing and a little frightening to realize just how powerful a memory, even one as early as this, can be. It is indeed a bit frightening, especially when you realize that today you are the one creating the memories of tomorrow.

The children are watching. They are listening. Make the memories count. Let them hear of Christ from your lips and see Christ in your life. Such memories will last forever.

Camping Out!

Mary and I have always loved camping. It doesn't really matter much to us whether we head to the beach or the mountains; we simply love the feel of camping along with the almost-instant camaraderie that develops amongst the tent, popup, trailer, and fifth-wheel folks. Even the land-yacht people say "Howdy!" when you pass by. It is almost as if social strata don't exist. It is truly wonderful. There are no liberals, no conservatives, no Catholics or Protestants, no rich or poor, no black or white. It is just us folks.

Refreshing is probably the best way to describe the feeling one receives upon setting up the camper, the grill, the picnic table, and the canopy, lowering the stabilizers, hooking up the water, the electricity, and the sewage pipe, all the while swatting a newly graduated class of mosquitoes. Yep, it must be the camaraderie.

Mary and I have owned several camping contrivances over the years. Like most folks we started tent camping, moved up to a pop-up, elevated ourselves to a pull behind, got uppity and bought a fifth wheel, uppity again and bought another fifth wheel, sold that so Uncle Sam could have his pound of flesh, and we are now on the far side of the hill working our way back down.

A few years ago, we purchased a 1976 Avion LaGrande camper. It is one of those pull-behind aluminum jewels. Truthfully the craftsmanship is first-rate. That being said, it was built the same year I graduated high school. I'm not saying it is all that old, but like me, it did have an issue or two when we bought it. One of those issues was a broken vent cover on the roof.

One day, when thunderstorms threatened above, I had to do something to fix the cover quickly to prevent a leak. So I gathered up some duct tape (thank God for duct tape!) and a plastic garbage bag.

As it turned out I had no ladder with me, so with an agility that belied my age, I climbed to the top of the camper Jackie Chan-style. I stepped on the tongue, then up on the propane tank, then onto the top of the front window awning, and then to the summit, the top of the camper. I quickly taped the plastic bag over the broken vent turned around and realized, much to my dismay, that while coming up was pretty easy, getting back down was well-nigh impossible. You see, the curved side of the camper aided in my ascent, but made my descent treacherous to say the least. I was in a pickle.

It was a pretty day, though, exclusive of the thunder and lightning, so I just sat up there on my perch and thought for a while. Finding no solutions, I thought some more. When I began to fancy that I would remain up there imitating the Sphinx indefinitely, a pickup truck happened by.

Having his interest piqued by the sight of my newfound treasure, the driver parked by the curb and came over to take a look. Apparently he had not seen me, because when I said "Good afternoon," that he was startled would be an understatement. He recovered quickly, though.

He was about my age and, apparently seeing nothing unusual about me sitting on top of the camper, he proceeded to tell me of an old Airstream he was fixing up, left to him by his father. That familiar camaraderie came into play quickly after that. When I sheepishly told him of my plight he laughed, as was his right, and then he parked his truck right next to the camper, climbed up on the roof, and helped me down.

I never asked his name, and he never asked mine. I don't know if he is a Methodist, a Baptist, or an Episcopalian. I haven't the foggiest idea of his political views. What I do know is that he had a dad who loved him and passed on the love of camping, and I know he helped me out of a tight spot.

My prayer is that as a Christian, I leave similar impressions behind when I depart. I pray that folks don't remember my politics, that I was Methodist, or that I fail to think ahead from time to time. My prayer is that folks remember I lived my faith, and that in a tight spot I offered a hand when it was needed. When comfort was called for, I offered a shoulder to cry on and an ear to listen.

I pray folks see Christ in my actions more than my words, and I pray the same for you.

The Walking Maple

Out of the early morning mist he materialized, for all the world like a phantom of folklore. As my eyes adjusted to the sight, the feathered edges became more distinct, the shadows lightened, and the silhouette of a man stood before me. He was some distance off but my eyes, sharpened by instinct, took in the fedora, the slightly stooped stance, the hooked nose, and what appeared to be a shotgun slung over his left shoulder.

It was early morning in the Congaree Swamp after a long night of rain, so the fog was dense, vision was uncertain, and the sounds of the swamp were alive with the hollowness that fog and cypress trees produce. As I took in the sight, I could hear the echoed cry of a whippoorwill in the distance, and the soft mysterious strains of a five-string banjo came to my mind.

As the distance closed between us, I first noticed the smile, followed by the laughing eyes. It would appear that my reaction was a bit amusing to this stranger. On his head was a hat more befitting a banker than a phantom, and instead of a Browning pump-action 12 gauge, on his shoulder rested a tripod with a Nikon D3 attached.

As it turns out, he wasn't amused by my reaction at all, but was himself startled almost to the point of panic by the bearded apparition standing before him.

"Nobody takes this trail," he said, "You 'bout scared me to death!"

I told him the feeling was mutual, we both laughed at ourselves, and then we fell to talking.

He was a really nice fella, somewhere around sixty, as wiry as they come, with a winning gap-toothed smile and a hair-trigger laugh. He told me he has lived in and around the swamp all his life and truly loves the place. He loves it to the point of wanting to share it with everyone, and on this particular morning, I was blessed to be the benefactor of his desire and knowledge.

As always, I had my Nikon strapped to my chest and a tripod hanging from my pack, and being kindred spirits, he said he had to show me something.

"Have you ever heard of a 'walking maple?'" he asked.

I answered in the negative, and he then exclaimed that just a short half of a mile off the trail was the finest example of a walking maple in the entire South. So off we went, slogging through the mud and the blackwater until we came to a little break in the woods where a quiet pond stood. My guide nodded toward a beaver lodge in the distance, to which the pond owes its existence, and then he motioned over the water drawing my attention to the far shore.

Standing on the shore—well, actually standing above the shore—was the "walking maple." A tree on stilts is the best way to describe it. It appears that from time to time an old cypress tree will die and snap off a few feet above the ground leaving a stump. In the course of time, a maple seed will come to rest on the stump and sprout. As the maple grows, it first seeks nutrition from the old stump, but soon the old wood is exhausted and offers no succor to the maple. Seeking solace elsewhere, the maple extends its roots over the edge and down the side of the old cypress stump and eventually finds rest and consolation in the rich soil of the swamp.

As the maple continues to grow, the now-exhausted cypress stump rots away but it does so gradually enough to afford the maple time to strengthen its roots to the point of withstanding its own weight. What is left is a maple tree standing a few feet off of the ground supported by nothing more than its roots.

It is an interesting sight to be sure, for the maple has no tap root to speak of, and in turn while its roots fan out around the now suspended tree, the center, beneath the tree, remains vacant.

It is a startling sight. It does indeed look like the tree is about to take a leisurely stroll.

My companion was beside himself as I marveled at this new discovery. He told me with a gleam in his eye that the old timers believed these trees would walk around at night guided by the light of the swamp gas and get into all sorts of mischief.

With that he said, "I only live a couple of miles from here and I need to head home. Just go back the way we came and you'll hit the trail in time."

He then shook my hand, and with a smile and a nod he disappeared into the mist once again. The banjo music slowly faded and the whippoorwill was alone once again, left to play his melancholy tune.

Why do I tell this story? Well, because I see a couple of quick lessons in it. First of all, life is an adventure. Overcoming your fears and venturing out through the swamp, or out for Christ, has its rewards.

Secondly, like the walking maple, we as Christians start out relying upon others for our spiritual sustenance: our parents, our Sunday school teachers, our pastors, and the like. In time, however, others will come to rely upon us. We had best be prepared to pass the spiritual DNA down to future generations, or they will be weaker as a result of our neglect.

So study and learn the Word of God, pray to Christ for strength and wisdom and an increasing faith, and be there for those who follow.

Boardwalk at Dusk, Congaree National Park, by Tony Rowell

Let Not Your Hearts

There are few activities I enjoy more than heading off all by myself to the woods and spending an afternoon hiking through the Congaree Swamp. I have been asked many times what draws me to such an activity. I usually strap something heavy on my back, I sweat, I swat mosquitoes that rival your average sparrow in size, I get thirsty, and I get tired. I have to beware of snakes, scorpions, and the occasional loud-mouthed hiker who has yet to grasp the idea that wildlife tends to shy away from loud obnoxious voices, and if I'm not careful, I could re-enact an old Burt Reynolds movie and never be seen again. So, you might ask, why the fascination?

Well, it's simple. The peace that resides in the swamp is marvelous.

Now, when I first arrive at the ranger station, there is usually a busload or two of grade-school children doing what such children always do: disturbing the peace. The pushing and shoving, the yelling and the excited voices of the few truly interested kids questioning their teachers and the rangers fills the air; and for someone seeking quiet refuge, the fight or flight instinct begins to rise to the surface.

Once I start down the boardwalk, however, the forest begins to dampen the voices of the children and the clamor of the outside world begins to fade. Then as I go farther in and leave the boardwalk behind to venture down one of the longer trails, which ninety-five percent of the visitors never experience, the world behind is swallowed by a palpable silence. As I proceed further, that silence morphs into a peace that, just an hour or so before, was thought unattainable.

Continuing on, the voices of the birds, the myriad sounds of the other wildlife, the whisper of the wind, and that mysterious undervoice of nature that I have never fully identified begin to envelop me. Then the peace that surrounds me moves in.

It is at the moment when the world seems a distant place and the towering trees remind me that I am but a small part of a grand scheme, that the still small voice of God can be heard. For me, the message of that voice is always the same. As I walk on, God whispers in my ear that the quiet of the moment is to be cherished, but that the peace is to be claimed.

Life is not always quiet. The voices that vie for our attention can be very insistent, and if we are not careful, a subtle panic can work its way into our souls. When that occurs, the promised peace of God becomes endangered by the incessant bawling of the world.

The temptation to listen to the world's wailing is strong. Giving into the urgency of the moment appears much more sensible than quietly waiting for and trusting the God of our fathers to bring His promised peace.

Nevertheless, trust requires patience, and patience requires trust.

Do you trust Christ? If you do, then claim His peace and be willing to wait in quiet confidence for that still small voice that carries it.

"Rejoice in the Lord always. I will say it again: Rejoice! Let your gentleness be evident to all. The Lord is near. Do not be anxious about anything, but in everything, by prayer and petition, with thanksgiving, present your requests to God. And the peace of God, which transcends all understanding, will guard your hearts and your minds in Christ Jesus" (Philippians 4:4-7).

Staggered Joints

Several years ago, I built a stone wall around a flower bed over at my cabin. The bed is somewhere between fifteen to twenty feet long and around ten feet wide, so it took me a little time to finish the thing. It was backbreaking work, and I soon discovered muscles in the back of my legs I had forgotten existed; but all in all it was a lot of fun. There is nothing like watching a wall rise where nothing existed before for positive reinforcement.

When you do this kind of work you usually do it alone, I have discovered. Family members tend to migrate to areas away from shovels and the like, and it is a good friend indeed who will mix mortar with you. In turn, I had time to think.

As I was working my way around the wall, I was following my training and subconsciously staggering the joints between the rocks. That is, I was not simply stacking the rocks one on top of another, but I was placing two rocks end to end on one level and spanning the joint between them with the rock above. In so doing I was making a very strong wall. Instead of making a wall of columns stacked beside one another, which is anything but stable, I was constructing a wall that was interconnected and therefore able to withstand the pressures of many years of use. I figure that wall will be there when I am long gone.

As I continued my work it struck me how the family of God is like that wall, or at least should be. I add the "should be" because all too often those of us who make up the body tend to balk a little at the idea of staggering the joints. To stagger the joints means we will have to rely upon someone else for support and strength. It means we will have to work with one another for the common good. It means compromise and consensus will need to be attained, and that means we just might have to give up a thing or two, and we don't like that. I know I don't!

That being said, for the body of Christ to present a united front to the world, we just might need to stagger a bit. Now this doesn't mean we will have to submerge our personalities or our opinions, for that matter. Trust me, that wall I built has all sorts of rocks in it, from sharp ornery ones to smooth gentle ones and every type of rock in between. Some of the rocks don't fit just right with their neighbors, but each and every one of them has found at least one point at which to make contact and continue the strength.

We must do the same in the church of Christ. While we may disagree on all sorts of things, from the color of the carpet to the translation of the Bible we use, our point of contact is Jesus Christ and His saving grace. From that point, the strength of the faith continues.

While we Christians tend to enjoy setting up various ministries and/or denominations, stacking them beside one another, and calling them the church, we must understand that to engage in such things tends to weaken, not strengthen, the church. A column with no support will soon fall. Only through the intermingling of all of our calls and the joining of our spirits will the church of Christ be strengthened and the Body made whole.

My challenge is simple. Let us all work together to build a wall of faith. With all of our strengths staggered and Christ as our mortar, it will be a joy to watch the wall rise.

Walking Maple (Congaree Swamp), by Tony Rowell

Drifting

I will never forget the late summer afternoon when my crazy Granny Tharpe proved that she was ahead of her time by having the top part of her left ear pierced. You know, just like all of the young folks do today. Only Granny did it way back in the mid-sixties long before it was cool.

It was different back then. It was a simpler time, to be sure. Back then only women, pirates, and a few unique people got their ears pierced. A lot of women didn't even bother to go anywhere to get it done. You know, back then they weren't so flighty about everything like we are today. They were not quite so particular about being sure everything was sanitary and the like either. They simply used a piece of ice to numb the earlobe and a sewing needle to do the deed. Tie some knots in the thread, and pull a knot through every day or so until it healed. It was as simple as that. But not my Granny, she was far too radical for that. So in keeping with her favorite pastime, my Granny used a number 10 fishing hook to pierce her ear.

To be honest, if the truth were told, Granny didn't actually do the deed. It was Grandpa who got the job done. And talk about radical—he didn't even have the courtesy to ask her before he did it.

It all happened right before sunset out on Deerpoint Lake about a half mile from the Lynn Haven Landing. We were in a couple of rented jon boats and, as I recall, Granny and Mike, my brother, were in one boat, and Grandpa and I were in the other. We had been fishing for bass and bream and anything else that would bite all afternoon with no luck at all. So about the time the sun was ready to set, when the wind dies down and the lake smooths out, Grandpa decided to try another tack. He reached under the seat and pulled out his fly rod and reel. He figured, like any good fisherman does, that if one thing doesn't work, you try another until you find the right combination that brings home the bacon (or bass, depending).

Now, my Grandpa was born to fish. A rod and reel in his hand felt honored to be there because in almost any situation that rod and reel were going to look good, and today was no exception. The only person with more grace than displayed by my Grandpa with a fly rod was his young prodigy, my brother, Mike, after he grew up, so instead of fishing I just settled back to watch and learn.

I received a good lesson in the art of fly fishing that day. I learned of the gentle strength that is needed to place that fly before the fish with only a faint ripple accompanying it. I learned of the mystical way that a true fly fisherman knows when the time is right to send that fly winging toward the prey. I watched as on the back stroke the line began to curl in upon itself and just before the opposing edges met they were snapped forward, straightened out and ever so gently placed upon the surface of the water. It is truly a beautiful thing to watch.

Well, while Grandpa was engrossed in his fishing and I was mesmerized in my watching, Granny and Mike were drifting. So in one of those quirks of fate, Grandpa—with the simple flick of his wrist—sent that number ten Marathon fly behind him, let it kinda rest in the air for a moment, and with another flick sent it careening through the air toward a particularly enticing ripple in the water at about a hundred miles an hour.

Somewhere in the middle of the stroke my Granny got her ear pierced.

Now, during World War II my Granny had worked in the shipyard as a welder, and about the time that hook hit home, she proved she was equal to the task of telling that fly and her husband exactly what she thought of the whole affair. It wasn't much, mind you.

As you may recall, my brother was on the boat with Granny, and it was about this time that he began to question Granny's moral authority for washing his mouth out with soap for saying "darn," but he decided it would be prudent to let it pass.

It was also about that time that both my brother and I began to develop a love for fly fishing. It looked like a whole lot of fun to a couple of young boys.

So what is the moral of this story? Simple: Be careful where you drift!

Great-Uncle Wilkie's Light

Let me tell you a bit about my Great-Uncle Wilkie. First and foremost, though, let me make it clear that he was my great-uncle by marriage. If I was blood kin to him, I would never admit it for fear of being banned from proper society.

Uncle Wilkie was indeed one of the foulest men I have ever met, and trust me, I have met a few. Now I know that, like all of us, he was created in the image of God, but trust me also when I say Uncle Wilkie's rendition of that image did not show off God's best side.

I was introduced to Uncle Wilkie on a rainy Sunday afternoon when I was just a little boy, and from then on I would fight tooth and nail to avoid going to his house again. I just didn't like him on sight, but from time to time, Granny and Grandpa Tharpe would be overtaken by guilt and familial obligation, and off we would go to the old ramshackle two-story house that sat behind the defunct football field and the accompanying defunct burned-down high school.

I think that old house was the only thing left of whatever town had once been there, because desolate doesn't begin to describe the place. I don't think it had ever seen a coat of paint, exclusive of the tobacco juice Uncle Wilkie had deposited along the bottom planks like some sort of gross pair of pantaloons.

Uncle Wilkie was skinny as a rail, cussed like a sailor, spat like a viper, and refused to wear a clean shirt most of the time. That is, when he wore a shirt at all. To this day I can still see that old sunken-in chest of his covered with those gray mats of hair.

It was the stuff that nightmares are made of in the mind of a little boy.

Uncle Wilkie was indeed an odd bird. One of his proclivities was that he hated electric light. Now, each room in the house had a single lightbulb hanging from a wire smack in the middle of the ceiling, but that old fella preferred the light of a kerosene lantern. Go figure. I suppose it reminded him of days gone by.

In his bedroom, the flickering light of a kerosene lantern was usually all the light to be found. And yes, the shadows dancing around helped secure Uncle Wilkie's creepiness.

Appearance aside, though, in some things he was particular. One was the quality of light that issued from his lamp. The wick had to be trimmed just so, or he wasn't happy, and that is where my Grandpa's sister, Carrie, came into play.

There is an old saying that you can't make a silk purse out of a sow's ear, but in one of the strangest relationships on record, you can marry a silk purse to a sow's ear and make it work.

Aunt Carrie was one of the sweetest, neatest, and nicest people I have ever met, and yet somehow she was saddled with Uncle Wilkie as a partner in life—and from all appearances, she was satisfied with the arrangement.

When I read the book of Job for the first time, I thought about Aunt Carrie and decided there had to have been a side wager between God and Satan, and Aunt Carrie was the prize. Nonetheless, Aunt Carrie loved that cantankerous old man and treated him like a king. Skinny or not, he was well fed with good old country-style Southern cooking, which for the record cannot be topped no matter how hard you try. The house was always spotless, exclusive of the tobacco stains she didn't get to in time.

I have seen that woman on her hands and knees trying to get a stain out that could have been avoided altogether had Uncle Wilkie had the courtesy enough to just walk outside or use a cuspidor.

I remember walking into the kitchen one afternoon and finding Aunt Carrie with her reading glasses down on her nose and her forehead all wrinkled in concentration. She was trimming away on a new wick in one of Uncle Wilkie's lanterns. I asked her what she was doing, and she told me she was getting the light right. I asked her what she meant, and she told me the only way to get good light out of a lantern was the trim the wick just so. She showed me one she had finished, and then she taught me how to do it.

You don't just trim it straight across. You make a little mountaintop out of it. She snipped and looked and snipped and looked until she had it just right. The sides of the trimming were Rocky Mountain steep, but the top looked like the Smokies, rounded off and smooth. I'll tell you, a computer couldn't have done a neater job than Aunt Carrie.

That night she showed me why she did it. She took one lantern and cut the wick straight across and lit it. The flame was all fits and starts and smoke. On top of that, the flame was blue for the most part. There is not much light in a blue flame. She put the glass over it, and it just got worse.

Then she lit the wick she had trimmed so carefully, and the difference was startling. The light was twice or three times as bright, and it was yellow. There is lots of light in a yellow flame. It smoked a bit, but then she put the glass over it, and that light increased another two or three times, the flame reached for the ceiling within the glass, and the smoke altogether disappeared.

That flame was perfectly shaped, even on both sides, and slightly curved at the top. You couldn't have done better.

Of course, Uncle Wilkie enjoyed the light, but he never said anything to Aunt Carrie. Not a thank you or anything, but she just smiled and went on with her business.

A few nights ago as I lay down, I asked the Lord what he wanted me to write about this time around. That night I dreamed about Uncle Wilkie and Aunt Carrie and the aforementioned wick.

Now, chances are the dream was a result of me eating seven pieces of French toast followed by an entire World's Best Chocolate Candy Bar as a chaser, but I took it as a sign nonetheless.

This world will seldom if ever offer thanks for the sacrifices you make. It matters not how high your flame reaches nor how beautiful your light shines for Christ. While the world may appreciate you and hold you up as an example, chances are it won't.

More than likely, it will simply enjoy the light, take warmth from its glowing, take guidance from its luster, and never consider its origin, but don't lose heart. Maybe, just maybe, a young child will see you as you are down on your hands and knees cleaning the mess of the ungrateful and be changed.

Maybe, just maybe, the light of Christ will flare up at just the right time to change a life. You never know, so keep on shining.

The Haitian Boy (2010)

When I first stepped off the little plane, the blast of tropical heat mixed with the underlying acrid odor of post-earthquake Haiti hit me like a brick wall. I had prepared myself for this, but for once, the reality was stronger than the anticipation, and a wave of fear went through me as the enormity of the situation became evident.

For the faint smell of death to still be in the air twenty days after the quake boggled the mind, but in the air it was, and as my mind began to truly grasp that fact, a sense of helplessness drove out the remaining remnants of fear.

That was my first impression of Haiti when we arrived. I had hoped for something different. Somehow while knowing the facts, I had convinced myself that once witnessed, the devastation would be less than anticipated; and as we drove toward Port-au-Prince, I began to think that it was a possibility. While many buildings were damaged, few were down on the way to the guest house, so as night fell I consoled myself with the memory of what I had and had not seen that afternoon.

After breakfast on Monday, however, we made our way to the remains of Port-au-Prince. There is truly no way to describe it adequately. I have photos, some pretty good of the destruction, but they only give a snapshot of the situation, just a grain of sand on the beach. As I stood amongst the rubble and realized there was nowhere I could turn or run to escape, it truly felt like an oppressive weight was placed upon me. I had an odd sense of breathlessness. Sounds contrived, I know, but I felt it nonetheless.

Like many in the ministry, I often feel the need to set things right again. From broken hearts to broken marriages, a large part of my life is spent trying to do just that. To mend fences and heal spiritual wounds is my stock and trade. When faced with any given situation, my instinctual reaction is to look for ways to make it right again. When faced with the image of the destruction of an entire city and the deaths of more than 250,000 souls, my reaction was, in all honesty, despair.

While I appeared for all intents and purposes to be handling things well, my heart was in utter turmoil. Finding Christ, much less doing His work in this horrible situation, seemed impossible. In all honesty, mentioning Christ and His promise of love seemed almost cruel in such a situation. What evidence was there of such a love, anyway? There was evidence of power. As I was shaken from my bed on two consecutive evenings, that power was undeniable. But love? Finding that was another matter altogether.

I found myself asking what my role was, if I had one at all, in God's plan here. For while I admit chaos was the only thing in evidence, I knew and still know God has a plan for His creation. I know no matter how dark life may appear, Christ is always near. Sometimes the darkness seems to blot out any evidence of Christ's presence, but faith does not require evidence. It simply requires knowing.

Late on Monday afternoon, after having driven for about seventy-five miles with no break in the devastation, we stopped at the remains of a little church to visit the local preacher and find out what, if anything, could be done to save the church buildings. As we entered the courtyard, we found ourselves in the midst of a tent city. It was one of thousands, for as the people fled their homes they set up shelters outdoors for fear of other quakes.

As the rest of the team went to examine the buildings, a young father, Michael, motioned for me to follow. As I did, he brought me to a makeshift tent. Linens, cardboard, and the like completed the structure. Once there, he introduced me to his young family: a lovely wife and a few kids. As I listened, he told me of the home he had lovingly built over three years, and how it had been destroyed in an instant. He didn't want sympathy; he just needed an ear.

As I listened to him, despair began to creep into my soul again. Not only mine this time, but his as well, as his entire life lay before him in an eight-by-five makeshift tent.

After he finished his story, he asked if I would pray with him. I tried to pray, but the words wouldn't come. How could my words—how could any words—bring comfort? So I just stood with him as he quietly cried. As I tend to do sometimes, I was overcome with emotion as well, and as Michael and I stood there lost in thought, I felt a little hand slip into mine. I opened my eyes and looked down, and a little boy of about ten was gently gripping my hand and looking up at me with such concern in his eyes that it broke my heart. His world had been destroyed. His life would never again be the same. And yet this little boy put all of that aside to try to bring comfort to, of all people, me.

As we headed back to Port-au-Prince late that afternoon, my despair was lessened and a light was dawning in my mind. Perhaps I didn't have to set it to rights. Perhaps my role, all of our roles in life, isn't so much to do what God would have us do as it is to be who God would have us be.

I fear that often I get lost in the ministry I perceive that the Lord has for me, when all He truly desires from me is love—love for Christ and love for the other folks on the road.

It's the same love I witnessed in the eyes of a little Haitian boy in the midst of the horror that had become his life here on earth: a love so pure it shined in his eyes.

The same love that shined in Christ's eyes in the midst of the horror that His life had become on Calvary: a love so pure, so amazing that He overcame all obstacles, even death, for the objects of that love.

Haitian Boy 2010, by Tony Rowell

People, Not Projects

A few weeks ago, I headed to Conway, South Carolina, to attend a Volunteer Organizations Active in Disaster meeting relating to recent fires down that way. As it turned out, I was the "old man" in the room. With my twenty-some-odd years of experience in missions and working disasters, I was by far the oldest guy, mission-wise at least, at the meeting.

As the computer screens flashed and the keyboards rattled, as the blackberries did whatever they do and a woman who could be my daughter explained the use of the latest electronic gadgets and how wonderful they are for communication in a crisis, I began to feel just a bit older than my fifty years. I began to wonder if my tired mind would be able to keep up with the latest advances in electronics as they relate to mission work and the like.

I thought back to my early days in the field when cell phones were only seen on Miami Vice and a computer was named Hal. I thought back to when phones had dials, houses had antennas, and schools had prayer. You know—back in the days when a hard drive meant you were heading cross-country with no air conditioning.

During a break in the meeting, I headed outside for a bit of fresh air and a moment or two to ponder all of this when my cell phone rang. I answered it. It was my Uncle Al, my dad's brother, telling me my father was on the way to the hospital, and it looked bad this time. A short time later, I received another call, from my sister, Janie, telling me Dad appeared to be gone. Finally, my sister-in-law, Laura, rang and gave me the news that indeed my father had gone to rejoin my mother, who'd left a short nine years ago.

As I traveled back down Highway 501 toward home, I kept replaying the conversations in my mind. Once again, I heard their voices. I heard the grief mixed with concern for me as I traveled, and I felt some comfort. I suppose all of our wonderful communication tools do have their place.

Comfort or no, I was still alone with my grief, and to say it was difficult would be the truth. To be alone at such a time is not a good thing.

When at last I made it home and gratefully hugged my lovely bride, Mary, the grief and pain were almost immediately halved. When Friday night arrived and I stood on tired feet for two hours shaking the hands of many folks who loved me and some who barely knew my name, the pain was lessened all the more. Then on Saturday, as I gathered and celebrated my father's life with others caught in the same grief, the shared sorrow lessened the load on all our hearts.

All too often we focus on all the wrong things. We focus on the bottom line. We focus on getting the job done and getting it done quickly and efficiently, and in so doing, we allow life and those God has placed on our paths to pass on by.

As you and I practice ministry, be it from the pulpit, in Bolivia, in Haiti, or down at the grocery store, let us never forget for whom we have been sent. Let us never allow the ministry to interfere with ministering.

We as missionaries are sent out to people, not to projects. While God may send us out to build a school dormitory, to rebuild a damaged church, or to raise an orphanage out of the dust, we are truly being sent out to share the love of Christ with the "least of these." To comfort the grieving, to help the helpless, and to lead the lost to Christ is why we do what we do.

Let us never lose sight of the purpose of our work: God's people.

The comfort of a touch, of a shoulder to lean on, of honest Christian concern, was brought home to me anew at the passing of my father. It is my prayer that I never forget the importance of such things.

It is my prayer that all of you never forget, as well.

Little One of Bolivia, by Tony Rowell

The Nation of "I"

"I don't know about you," said the older man with the crow's feet around the eyes and the gray feathering its way through his temples, "but I am about as tired as I can be of the morals flaming out around me. It seems to me no matter where I turn, the rights and wrongs have gotten all twisted up. I mean, when I was a chap, none of this catting around would be put up with, especially not in the high places; but now it seems nobody cares anymore about anything or anybody but themselves. 'If it don't bother me, who cares?' That's what they say. Darn fools."

He shifted a bit in his seat to keep this part or that from falling asleep, then dove back into his attack.

"I think I know what the problem is. I think I know why we're in such a fix, and I think I know how to cure it. You see, it's like this. We are all alone out there. We sit around, side by side, and don't even talk to each other. We fuss that the morals of this great country are headin' south, and nobody's listening. If I've heard it once, I've heard it a thousand times: 'Those politicians and judges are taking my morals and my God and throwing Him and them in the trashcan, and I don't know what to do about it. I try to raise my kids right, but the schools and the TV try to raise 'em wrong and win most of the time. What's a fella to do?' That's what I hear, and I think I know where we're going wrong.

"You see, it's like this. Back in my day, just before the Great War, we were all do-ing pretty well. Yeah, we heard about the war in Europe and all, but that wasn't us. That was them, and what were we supposed to do about it? Now some among us had kin over there, and they would cry out that their kinfolk were being killed and we needed to do something to help.

"Now we weren't about to go get ourselves killed for their kinfolk. They weren't our kinfolk. They were their kinfolk, so let them go die for them, not us. But one day, December 7, as I recall, the Japanese flew into Pearl Harbor and bombed our boys. They killed our people. They attacked us. Now it wasn't their kinfolk, it was our kinfolk being killed, and we had to do something about it.

"On account of that horrible day, though, something strange and wonderful happened. Because of Pearl, we came to life. There weren't no more blacks or whites or men or women. There was just us, and we had to do something to protect our nation and our people. In the flash of a torpedo we turned from a nation of 'I' into a nation of 'we.' It wasn't 'I' have had it with Hitler and his crowd, it was 'we' have had it, and after that, we knew we were going to win. After the I became we, we had them. Multiply that 'we' a million times, and there was no stopping us.

"Now, we haven't had a Hitler to deal with for a while now, and like men have always done, we've fallen to our old ways. We are once again a nation of I: I want my rights. I want my way. I want to do whatever I darn well please, thank you, and I don't care what you or God or anybody for that matter has to say about it.

"But, friend, my God and my morals are under attack just as sure as Pearl was, and so are yours. And unless we come together, not as black men and women or white men and women, but simply as men and women all created in the image of God to fight the forces of evil, which have the upper hand in this great nation of ours, it appears the United States of America will sink just as sure as did the Arizona.

"It's high time we stop letting the forces that rule the airways and the government tear at the fabric of our nation and at our God.

"When they take prayer out of my school, they take it out of yours. When they say the murder of infants is OK in my town, they say it is OK in yours. When they attack me and my beliefs, they attack you and yours, and until we come together as one, to stand up to the evil forces that try to divide us, the destruction will continue. Until we can stand side by side as one, against the forces of selfish desire and immorality, such things will continue to flourish. Until we link hearts and minds and proclaim in one voice, 'We have had enough,' this great nation of ours will continue to decay until there is nothing left but the aftermath of evil."

For a moment, he looked a bit bewildered, then he shifted in his seat once more to relieve this part or that, and with tired eyes he stared out across the crowded Applebee's and sighed a sigh of resignation with the shadow of fear and longing crossing his weatherworn face.

That old man and I sat next to one another waiting on a table in Applebee's way back in 1998. I had never met him before, but he asked me what I did for a living, and when the word "preacher" came out of my mouth, his bomb-bay doors opened and out came his story.

I feel sure he is long gone now, but the truth of his words remains.

I don't know about you, but I love this country. To quote Merle Haggard, "If you're putting down my country, man, you're walking on the fighting side of me."

You see, I have been blessed, as many of you have, to see a great deal of the rest of the world, and trust me, there is no place I would rather live than right here in the good old U.S. of A. It is truly the greatest nation to ever grace the planet, but we are in danger.

As love of God and country is being, and in many cases has been, replaced with love of self, the decay has indeed continued. As we near the tipping point, it is time that we as brothers and sisters in Christ and fellow Americans stand shoulder to shoulder against the forces that would destroy this wonderful country of ours.

So wear the red, white, and blue proudly. Sing the anthem with enthusiasm and pride. Pray for our wonderful country and those who lead it, and do so in public. Let the world see you are unashamedly Christian and you are proud of the nation in which you live.

I am amazed when I think that simply writing these words of God and country will be considered radical by some, when to me they are just good old ordinary common sense (a rare commodity these days).

Thoughts from the Byways

Over the years, my childhood memories have taken on an amber hue. When I recall my days as a boy, I think of the fishing trips with Granny and Grandpa, the first runs of I Love Lucy and The Andy Griffith Show, the rides on Grandpa's Borden milk truck, and those great chinaberry trees in Granny's yard just made for climbing. I think of hiking with my dad in upstate New York and wandering through Cades Cove, Tennessee, with the family. I think of all the good things and the blessed moments of which one's memories should be made.

I don't think of the Bay of Pigs or the Cuban missile crisis. I don't think of Nikita Khrushchev and his shoe or Lee Harvey Oswald. Korea, Vietnam, and Kent State don't really factor into the memories of my childhood, and I suppose that is how it should be.

As one gets a bit older, though, things such as the state of the world begin to weigh upon you a little more as you think of the lives your children and their children will lead after you're gone. It is easy to get so caught up in the worry of things as they are and the imaginings of things to come that you forget to focus on the things of God and the great blessings He has bestowed upon you now.

This was brought home to me a few years back when Mary and I took a trip to Niagara Falls for our thirtieth wedding anniversary. Instead of rushing to the falls and the accompanying crowds, Mary and I took the long way around and wandered up through North Carolina, Virginia, West Virginia, Pennsylvania, and New York, and back through New York, Pennsylvania, Ohio, Kentucky, Tennessee, and North Carolina. We avoided the busy roads and ventured through small-town America. Somewhere along the way, I was able to leave the worries of everyday life behind and open my eyes to a reality that I knew to be true, but had failed to fully realize.

That reality has several levels, the first of which was a rekindled appreciation for the gift of my wife and family. Thirty years, make that thirty-five years now, of marriage makes for more than a few topsy-turvy moments in life. But looking back, I realize no matter what whirled about us, my family has held firm. There might be a few loose nuts on some of the bolts, but as a whole we've kept it together pretty well. I am greatly blessed.

Another aspect of this reality began to dawn upon me when I realized that no city, town, or country byway was without a steeple. As we traveled, the number of churches we saw was astonishing. If you listen to the news media these days, you might begin to wonder if Christ has any place left to lay His head in today's world. Well, I discovered He does. He rests in the hearts of many an everyday American as they quietly go about their lives, making memories for their children and grandchildren to cherish.

Finally, the reality of the strength of this great nation of ours was made clear to me on that trip. As we traveled from Gilbert to Punxsutawney and beyond, the Stars and Stripes were proudly displayed on homes and businesses and town squares from South Carolina to the northern border, and I was greatly heartened on account of it.

While we may disagree on a lot of things, it appears most of us do love this wonderful country in which we have all been blessed to live our lives.

As hard as it was for me to admit even to myself, I came to realize that some, perhaps many, of those beautiful flags so proudly displayed on all of those homes had probably not been placed there by folks who agree with me on all things. That being said, agree or not, we are all Americans.

As we enjoy our fireworks, celebrations, and red, white, and blue, we need to be truly thankful to our God above for the nation in which we live.

We may have our faults. We will have our disagreements. But no matter what "they" say, to be privileged to live in our "one nation under God" is a blessing for which we should be truly thankful.

Off the Beaten Path

I half expected to run headlong into a mastodon. The little valley I found myself in actually appeared to be that untouched, that pristine.

It was early May several years ago when I first discovered this treasure. I had noticed something on the map that intrigued me. So I figured the coordinates, picked up my compass, and took off through the swamp. What tickled my fancy was the Dead River Valley located about seven miles or so south-southeast off the sharp right turn in the King Snake Trail as it heads back into the park—the Congaree National Park.

If you continue in a straight line past the turn, you will eventually run into the Congaree River, provided of course that you can see the signs of an old rutted road that once carried loggers out of the swamp toward home. But if you veer off a bit to the left, say at about at a thirty-degree angle or so, and keep going until you think you're there, and then go half that far again, you will come to the Dead River Valley and the Dead River Lake. It is like stepping back into another time.

There is a holy, almost sacred feel to the place. When the undergrowth thins out before you and the cypress and tupelo come together to form a canopy above, the hush of the place seems to envelop you. You know, or at least I knew, God was there. I was in a safe place. I was able to speak freely with my Lord, and the world was far enough away that the still, small voice that is God could be heard.

Oh, the wind worked its way through the treetops giving voice to that mysterious, almost baleful, sound that carries within it the whispers of the past. The birdsong rebounded and echoed from cypress to cypress through the ever-present mist, coming from everywhere and nowhere it seemed, and yet the silence of the place filled me with peace and brought such a blessing.

The Congaree Swamp is a magical and mysterious world. If you listen closely, you can sometimes hear the faint echo of Sherman's cannons or the staccato cadence of a denizen long-forgotten held within the memories of the ancient trees. The cypress knees take on a life of their own at dusk and at dawn. It is in those moments of half-light that you see and hear things that breed apprehension and fear. Few are the folks who venture off the beaten path to discover the wonders within, and therefore few are the folks who receive the gifts offered there.

How often do we miss out on the blessings of God because of our fear of the unknown? Can we even count the times we have refused to venture forth for Jesus Christ because of imaginary dangers? Why is the well-worn path so appealing to the human being?

We are given but one life to spend as we wish on this earth. Why do we insist upon wasting so much of the gift hiding in the darkness when we could be basking in the Light?

I fear we simply don't trust the Light. We have lived in the familiar darkness so long that the Light frightens us, so in darkness we remain.

The blessings of God are only found when we venture out of the darkness and into the light of Christ. Only after we break the chains of fear are we blessed. So my challenge to each and every one of you is that you release your hold on the darkness, break the chains of your fear, and venture forth for Christ.

Petticoat Junction

A few years back on Good Friday, several tornadoes worked their way through our fair state doing a great deal of damage. Because the damage was scattered, a lot of us didn't know about it, but because of my work with disaster relief for the church, I was aware. So on Monday morning, I took a tour of the devastation.

The Early Response Team program of South Carolina was just getting off the ground back then. In that the ministry fell under my purview as chair of the United Methodist Volunteers in Mission-South Carolina, I wanted to see how they were doing in their work. I also needed to assess what further work was needed to get those folks affected by Mother Nature's rampage back on their feet again.

It was during my drive down near Aiken, Beech Island to be exact, that I came across a little community extensively damaged by an F2 tornado that had focused its fury upon it. Some of the homes were heavily damaged, but still standing. Some were completely blown away, and a few looked pretty good, exclusive of some minor roof damage. Nonetheless, the community itself was so desperately affected that it was indeed a miracle that it recovered. The name of the community is Petticoat Junction.

In spite of the destruction and loss those folks suffered, the federal and state governments decided not enough people were adversely affected by the tornadoes to offer any aid and assistance. No aid whatsoever was rendered to the families that lost their homes, their livelihoods, and their sacred mementos. The Federal Emergency Management Agency and the state have a complicated equation that is used to determine such things, and Petticoat Junction simply did not fit into the equation.

While I may consider that process flawed, I suppose you have to have some way to figure out such things, and I do believe they do the best they can. But what do folks in need do when the government leaves them high and dry?

They do what people at the end of their rope have always done: They call upon Christ and His church, and as always, Christ's church responds. It took a while, but between the Methodists, Baptists, and a few Mennonites, that community was brought back to life again—not for glory or fame, but simply because Christ has taught us to help those in need. Call it the Good Samaritan syndrome if you wish, but when all else fails, the faithful don't.

As I was driving home from Aiken that evening, my mind kept flashing back to one of my favorite television shows when I was a kid. You guessed it: Petticoat Junction.

My mind drifted back to the old Shady Rest Hotel, Uncle Joe, and those three pretty sisters peeking out over the top of the water tower. As I drove, I became homesick, and I began to pine for the time when television consisted of shows that were, for the most part, wholesome—a time when traditional Christian values were still viewed with respect and Christian living was still a sought-after commodity. I hungered for those days when we as a nation and as a church stood firmly on the side of Christ and His teaching about home and family, about right and wrong, about love and respect. My mind wandered back to a time when we, as Christians, were more concerned with what Christ taught than we were with what the prevailing culture thought.

It is amazing what can happen to a neglected culture in fifty-some-odd years, isn't it?

Petticoat Junction, Uncle Joe, and the girls are gone now, blown away by the forces of secularism, the me-first society, and an unhealthy desire to please folks at the expense of preaching the Gospel of Christ.

Right and wrong have been replaced with "whatever suits you," good and bad with "if it feels good, do it." It will be a miracle if our culture survives.

In spite of the damage done, the government will not step in to help in the cultural recovery. All too often, those in power make matters worse, anyway. So what are we supposed to do?

Well, I suppose there is nothing left to do but roll up our collective Christian sleeves and get to work. If we claim to be Christians, we need to start acting like it. We need to begin rebuilding the cultural foundation that has been undermined by those who would scoff at the Word of God.

We must find the courage to stand for Christ and Christ alone at every opportunity. We must defend His teaching with no fear of the world and no thought of retreat.

It won't be easy. To stand for Christ and His values places us in the crosshairs of a world that would rather destroy the messenger than accept the truth. That being said, we cannot back down.

Christ Jesus stood up for us to the point of being nailed to a cross. Today the time has come for you and me to stand for Him with similar courage. If we fail to stand as individuals and as a church, then the cultural bloodstain will fall upon us, and a nation built upon truth and justice may very well become a footnote in history.

I challenge all of us to live for Christ in a world where such a life is ridiculed. I challenge all of us to stand for Christ when the winds of unhealthy change blow across the nation. I challenge all of us to live for Christ no matter the consequences. I challenge you, and I challenge me, to call upon the Holy Spirit for the courage to stand up for Christ Jesus just as He stood for each and every one of us.

We must never retreat or surrender. Our children, our grandchildren, and their children yet unborn will benefit or suffer from what we do or don't do today.

Old Pump, by Tony Rowell

Memories (Granny's Banana Pudding)

Throughout most of the years of my adult life, I have been on a quest. I have searched far and wide. I have traveled the globe and tasted the creations of the masters.

As a modern-day Marco Polo of culinary delights, I have enjoyed balut and aso adobo in Manila, llama in La Paz, borscht in Moscow, rice and beans and beans and rice and rice and beans casserole in Costa Rica, plantains galore in Panama, armadillo in Colombia, guinea pig in Ecuador, prickly pear in Mexico, potatoes aplenty in Latvia, "strange meat" in Lithuania, (I promise that was the name of it), conch in Saint Croix, and I have feasted on the unknown in Montserrat.

Yet in all my searching and all my travels, I have never tasted anything as wonderful, as mysterious, or as satisfying as my Granny Tharpe's home-cooked banana pudding.

Some have come close. Mary, my lovely bride, comes the closest, but nothing quite matches the taste, texture, and ecstasy of Granny's banana pudding. There was just something about her pudding that made it the best.

Perhaps it was the crucible that contained her gastronomic wonder: a rectangular dish of chipped Pyrex with rounded corners and little glass ears upon which to grasp. The outside was the color of caramel and it was slightly translucent. Complementing the interior, there were little cream-colored flowers that danced across the outside surface.

Perchance she used goat milk or something more exotic. Maybe she had a secret banana supplier known only to her. Who knows, whatever, there was something special about it, some special ingredient that made it just right.

I will never know. The recipe died with her. She never shared it. My mom, being her closest genetic match, tried to duplicate the feat, but failed dismally.

I used to theorize that Granny's special ingredients consisted of a dash of orneriness and a splash of lard, considering the fact that in the Deep South, lard was and still remains a certified food group. I stand by that thought. But while lard lingers, Granny's special brand of orneriness will never be duplicated.

So I suppose her miraculous offering to the world of the culinary arts will remain in my memory forever. It will never pass my lips again this side of heaven, but my first Sunday dinner beyond the Jordan will be a delight.

Now I know chemically speaking my Granny's banana pudding may very well be the same as your Memma's, Mimmi's, or Grammie's offering to the world, but I will contend until the rapture and beyond that my Granny's is the best.

Now if you're itching for a fight, you are welcome to say otherwise. I wouldn't recommend it though, because somehow the essence, the very lifeforce of my Granny was in every Nilla wafer, every slice of banana, and every ladle of that luscious pudding that felt like satin on your tongue.

Memories are a gift from God, and they are amazingly powerful.

I would like to put forth this challenge. Throughout your life, do your best to make memories that will last. Memories, that when recalled, build up and strengthen your brothers and sisters in Christ.

Let your following of Christ be an inspiration to others, both young and old, Christians and nonbelievers alike. Let your life be such that when your time on earth is over you can look back and remember with humble pride the accomplishments made for the Kingdom and the King.

May the essence, the very lifeforce of Christ our Lord and Savior, be evident in all you do, every word you speak, and everything you are.

Grandpa and the Blues Harp

I can't recall the exact date. The best I can figure, it must have been somewhere around the middle of June back in 1967 or thereabouts. I was eight years old at the time, spending the summer months with Granny and Grandpa Tharpe. As I recall, it was a pretty morning. The sky was a beautiful deep blue, almost cobalt, and there were soft cotton-ball clouds floating in it. I remember it like it was yesterday, for some reason.

I also remember what I was doing at the time. I was standing between my Grandpa and Granny in front of Grant's Department Store in Panama City, Florida, throwing a world-class fit. Eight-year-olds have a gift for such things, you know.

I had plenty of them; fits, I mean. Hysterics were one of my best things. For the most part, I can't remember what set me off, but I do recall the genesis of this particular outburst. Of all things it was a Hohner Blues Harp in the key of E, and it was as shiny as a brand-new penny.

At the time of my ill-tempered outburst, it was displayed in a glass case just inside the front door and a little to the left near the jewelry counter, and I wanted it. I wanted it bad.

For those of you unversed in the subject, a Hohner Blues Harp is a harmonica, or French harp or mouth organ depending upon the region from which you hail. I could go into the difference between a chromatic model and a diatonic model, but there's no need. If you blow air through the thing, it makes music. Check that—sometimes it just makes noise.

My desperate desire for this particular instrument at this particular time in my life stems from a couple of things. In the early summer of 1967, "Branded Man" by Merle Haggard had just hit the charts, and along with that a fella by the name of Charlie McCoy had just released his first album. These days they would call it a CD or MP3 or STP or something like that, but back then it was an album, a black vinyl platter with grooves cut in it for the needle to ride along in. The sound wasn't perfect, but then again, what is?

Charlie McCoy was the best harmonica player to ever come down the pike, bar none, and Merle Haggard, God rest his soul, was created by God above to write and sing country music.

In the summer of '67, my young heart fell in love with two things: a little blond girl down the street by the name of Brenda and country music. I have no idea what ever happened to Brenda, but country music—real country music, that is, not today's stuff but the real McCoy—remains a love of mine.

At eight years of age, my fingers were not long enough to wrap around a banjo's neck, much less a guitar's, and I hated taking piano lessons. So I figured, why not get an orchestra that fits in your pocket?

I wanted to learn how to play the harmonica like Charlie, and I needed that Blues Harp to make it happen. I wanted it enough to fight for it, to demand it, to throw myself on the floor for it. After all I was a budding superstar, and I needed it.

I figured Granny and Grandpa would see the amazing potential within me and just buy it for me. After all, I was their favorite, Granny said so, and on account of that, I figured I deserved it. I was entitled.

But in a shocking turn of events, my Grandpa looked down at me with unwavering eyes and a note of finality in his voice and simply said, "No." At that, my ranting and raving began.

It was in the midst of my tirade when I experienced something I had never experienced before, and I vowed to never experience again. My soft-spoken and tender Grandpa spoke harshly to me.

He looked down at his woe begotten grandson, listened intently to my ever-increasing pity party, and said the following—gently, of course, as was his manner, but with just enough steel in his voice to make me shut my mouth and tremble. He said:

"Son, do you think I owe you something? If you are thinking that, then you are way off base. If you want that thing, then you will have to earn it."

Six weeks later, three days before I was to head back up to Utica and Mom and Dad, after what seemed like a mountain of chores, I was once again standing in front of Grant's Department Store with my Grandpa on another beautiful summer's morning.

He stopped me right before we went into the store, stooped down, and gave me the money I had earned to buy that harmonica. He didn't even go inside. He let me buy it all on my own.

I have to tell you, I was the proudest eight-year-old boy in all the deep South that morning—not because of the brand-new Blues Harp in the key of E that lay in my pocket, but because I had earned it. I had been given the gift of anticipating it, and I did it all by myself.

Now friends, that is how to teach a life lesson.

Parents and grandparents alike, I urge you to resist the world's misguided teaching and foolish ways. Teach your children the value of hard work, patience, personal achievement, and excellence. Let them work for their dreams. If you don't, then you will steal their dreams from them. Dreams are made of anticipation, not immediate gratification.

Christ has given you a formidable task: the task of raising godly men and women in an ungodly world. Teach them to have confidence in themselves, in their abilities, and in their intellect. But over and above that, teach them of Jesus Christ, of His love for them and His pride in them. Give them all the support you can, and then give them the firm foundation of a relationship with Jesus Christ, and they will be blessed beyond measure by you.

Granny Tharpe   Grandpa Tharpe

Tasi

I sat a little back from the group, watching. My chair had one front leg a bit shorter than all of the others, so I had to lean back on two legs to keep motion sickness at bay. This set me back just enough to observe without interfering too much. It also gave me the proper vantage point and just enough cover to pull out my Nikon with the 55-200 lens attached and take some sly shots of folks when they weren't aware.

For those unfamiliar, proper photography is not a matter of ISOs, F-stops, and white balance. It is so much more than proper composition, lighting, and lenses. True photography is greater than getting a moment in time down on film, or digitized as the case may be. Photography is a thing of the soul. A true photographer doesn't take pictures; they capture emotions and moods, the things of the spirit.

A posed photograph is good for posterity and remembrance, but a photo taken at the moment the mask comes down is art. Now the mask can be worn by fellow human beings or Mother Nature for that matter, but the mask, the walls we so carefully build, often hide the true beauty of the soul within.

In this particular case, my soul-searching was made easier by the surroundings and the company kept.

I was leaning back in that old red leatherette chair while sitting in the upper room of the tiny Tasi United Methodist Church. Tasi UMC sits about six or seven kilometers down a dusty, dirty, shake-you-till-your-fillings-fall-out dirt road, way out in the countryside of Latvia.

Latvia, by the way, is an absolutely beautiful country. From the regal cities filled with architecture to dazzle the eyes, to the beautiful countryside filled with ancient farm houses, picturesque outbuildings, and charming people to warm the heart, Latvia is an oasis of peace in a world filled with chaos.

Nesting in the middle of that countryside is Tasi UMC. As is true of most Soviet-era structures, the building that houses the church is somewhat nondescript. Intentionally built to promote sameness and discourage individuality, the old brick building projects a cool lifelessness at first impression. That impression, however, belies the warmth and life to be found in the upper right quadrant of the place—for it is there where a small but Spirit-filled group of believers meets for worship and fellowship.

We, a United Methodist Volunteers in Mission team, had come to help in any way requested. You never know on these trips what exciting treasures await you or what type of work you will be taking on. The work is seldom what is expected, and the treasures often arrive unanticipated, which makes them cherished all the more.

The Tasi church had been blessed to obtain the downstairs flat underneath the current worship space. They were working toward making it a safe gathering place for the entire community. Our task was to form and pour the concrete floor to begin the process of renovation.

It was the second Sunday we were there. After a truly delightful worship service, we had a lovely time of fellowship with the small congregation. The room for the fellowship was a little tight, though, so it took a bit of effort for everyone to fit in. But to the sound of scraping chairs, laughter, and the occasional "Pardon me, are you OK?," we all managed to get in there. A table had been set with cake, cookies, coffees, and other delights. We all sat down intermingled, personal space a thing of the past. We joked and laughed together, broke cake and cookies together, drank coffee together, and together we did a creditable impression of the Tower of Babel. It was wonderful beyond words.

Because of a couple of late arrivals, and my father's admonition that you always give a lady your seat, I found myself slightly out of the circle nesting in that old red leatherette chair with the bum leg. I had the perfect vantage point to witness joy and love as they emerged and formed.

The expressions and the feelings ran the gambit. The old hands, those folks who have gone with me forever it seems, were wide open with fully exposed hearts drinking in the joy and giving the Holy Spirit free rein. Others, newer to the trade, sat and pondered the emotion and Spirit-filled atmosphere of that little place and wondered where they fit in. They struggled with the mask as it slipped from its moorings exposing perhaps more than was comfortable. Our Latvian friends held the same expressions as did we. Some excited, some expectant, some cautious and some pensive, but all joyous.

I was sitting just out of the current, observing, when an older woman of the congregation caught my eye. I can't recall her name, to my sorrow, but she was the artist, the musician, the hippie of the church. Her hair was long, gray, and slightly disheveled, her gaze a bit unfocused, her dress brighter than all the others, and she was wise. She made space on the bench beside her and motioned for me to come and sit with the crowd. She then gently took my camera and laid it aside.

What a blessing it is to be loved.

Free from observing, free from leading, free from the mask, I allowed myself to blend into that joyous group, and what a tonic it was. It was a soul-freeing moment and a gift from God for which I will forever be thankful.

I wish the same for all of you.

The Venerable Old Cedar

If any of Eden remains, it can be found in the western quadrant of the Smoky Mountains somewhere along the hiking trails that hover above a place that goes by the name of Cades Cove. As a child my family would make the trek up to the Smokies every other year or so, and the high point of every trip was a ride around the Cades Cove loop.

The loop is an eleven-mile-long ribbon of single-lane blacktop that follows the boundaries of this magical place filled with wildlife unafraid of humans and fields filled with wildflowers unnumbered. The beauty of the place is breathtaking, and a drive around the loop will leave passersby filled with inexpressible awe at the loveliness produced by our Creator's hand.

But if the peace of Cades Cove is to be found, one must rise above. If a quiet soul is what you seek, then you have to take a hike.

As you ascend the northern slopes of the mountains surrounding the Cove and gaze down onto the fields of bachelor buttons and sour weed, then look up and out beyond the poplar and pine windbreaks that trace their ordered way across the fields, the distant mountains appear dreamlike through the ever-present mist. When you reach the place where the mountains begin to melt into the clouds, the white noise of life slowly fades away until nothing but the frantic sound of your heart beating, the rustling of the leaves above, and the still, small voice of God comes to your ear. It is then that the peace of Eden can be found. For me, at least, a hike through the Smoky Mountains is a quiet walk hand-in-hand with my Lord in the cool of the evening.

Yes, if any of Eden remains, it can be found along the hiking trails above Cades Cove.

My mom, Bobbie Jean by name, loved this place more than just about anywhere else in the world, save the backroads and black waterways of the Florida Panhandle, her home. The otherworldly wildness of the place seemed to fan an ancient fire within her Native American roots that simply smoldered at other times. Her emerald-green eyes would dance with excitement, and her voice would take on a lilting quality as she told us kids of the history of the place. You couldn't help but fall in love with the Cove when Mom spoke of it, for her love was contagious.

Mom did have one strange peculiarity when it came to this place. Like a mother with a favored child among many, she loved one particular tree in the cove over and above all others. It was a massive cedar standing alone and proud in a field on the northernmost border.

The tree had a presence about it that drew your eye and a quiet solitude that threatened melancholy if you looked upon it too long, not unlike my mother in many ways. There was a connection there, mystical and mysterious.

Just before her death, Mom asked me to take some of her ashes and place them at the base of that tree. So the summer after her passing I did just that. Veering off the trail, I stealthily made my way through the field in which that tree stood until I was beneath that venerable old cedar. Mom's law-and-order child breaking the rules to fulfill her final wish. I bet she wondered if I would do it, but love compelled me on, only to discover her final wish was for me.

As I turned up and tapped the bottom of that old Ball Mason jar, a fitting container for a country girl, the continuity of life became clear to me. My Native American roots found voice, and somewhere within my spirit, the mystical harmony of life and death and earth and heaven softly soothed my soul, and I was finally at peace with Mom's passing.

My Lord promised her eternal life. I knew she was at peace and content, and I was OK.

Dad passed away several years after Mom, and being a romantic at heart, I decided to place a portion of his ashes beneath that same old tree. So later in the summer after his passing, in the midst of a rainstorm, I retraced my steps and found myself beneath that old cedar once again. Sheltered from the rain by the outstretched limbs, I turned up and tapped the bottom of my Dad's jar, and Mom and Dad were reunited once again.

My folks loved each other passionately, and with passion comes fire, but little did I know how enduring that fire could be.

I returned to Cades Cove the very next summer to rekindle my memories and to find the peace, once again, that I had allowed to fade. My heart longed for that tree; somehow it had come to represent my folks, their relationship, and their love.

As Mary and I followed the loop, my anticipation grew. After what seemed like ages, I could at last see the afternoon sunlight slanting across the blacktop indicating the meadow was just up ahead.

Mary was the first to see it, and she fell silent, wondering no doubt what my reaction would be. As I recall, through my astonished haze, a laugh, a deep and satisfying belly laugh, rumbled up and out of me for all the world to hear.

You see, between the time of the reuniting of Mom and Dad and my return, a well-placed streak of lightening had split that tree in equal halves and burned it to the ground. "Blew it to smithereens," as Mom would say. I have to admit, though, that the smoldering remains were a fitting testimony to a wonderful couple with a fiery relationship and a fierce love.

I returned just a few months ago to the cove and took note of the stump. It has been years, but life remains. There was a hint of green and the beginning of a new venerable old cedar for future generations to admire.

I often wonder why the Lord draws certain memories out of me, why He wants certain things to remain between Him and me, and why He wants others told. Well, this time I think I may have an inkling.

The world is in turmoil. Every day it seems a new horror awaits us, and it fills us with dread and fear. Stability, it appears, is a thing of the past, and now even our beloved denomination has joined in the fray. The goings on as of late have left many of us concerned as to what direction things may take. The security of like minds and like spirits has vanished, it seems, leaving many afraid and unsure.

When I recall that old stump, I remember a majestic tree standing sentinel for decades. Countless storms assailed it. Winters too many to count burdened its limbs with snow. Untold birds raised their young and sent them soaring from its branches, while other creatures sought the shelter and coolness of its shade.

Then in an instant it was gone, through happenstance or providence we will never know. But take heart, for from the smoldering remains, new life emerged. Life cannot be defeated. Life will always find a way.

So take heart!

Matthew 16:18: "And I say also unto thee, That thou art Peter, and upon this rock I will build my church; and the gates of hell shall not prevail against it."

The Venerable Old Cedar (Cades Cove), by Tony Rowell

Steppin' Out!

Angel sat across from me in the old open-air passenger Jeep as we tore through the streets of Cali, Colombia. The Jeep had a brand-new coat of candy apple red paint adorning its sides, but try as he might, the driver couldn't hide the battle scars and near misses that traced their way down the fenders and side panels of the old rattletrap. The windshield bore a striking resemblance to a spider web shimmering in the early morning sun, and to say the tires lacked tread would be rather generous. But gracious, how that thing could move. As my Granny would say, it ran like a scalded dog through the streets, and you had best be prepared for the ride if you knew what was good for you. It was a hold-onto-your-hat, hang-on-for-dear-life type of ride, and I loved every minute of it.

The fact that the driver was named Christian and his navigator Angel seemed strangely comforting to me, but that did not appear to have an equal effect on the team's newbies, if their startled screams and hasty prayers were any indication. The thing was standard transportation for mission work, though, so I quietly prayed the new folks would embrace the adventure and increase their faith to the point of enjoyment.

During a brief lull in the excitement, I shouted over to Angel a question. You see, this candy apple red piece of greased lightning we were strapped into had intrigued me a little. For the life of me, I couldn't decide what make it was, so I asked Angel, who had manufactured the thing. His reply was equally intriguing. He said, "What part?" Then he proceeded to give me a brief genealogical history of the vehicle.

The engine was an International, the frame was from a Chevy, the body from a Jeep, the transmission was from some Korean company, and the tires were Michelins, of course. He proclaimed that last little tidbit with a sarcastic smile.

Upon reflection, the hodgepodge we were riding in seemed strangely fitting for mission work to me, but after he had finished, I realized he had missed something, so I asked him who manufactured the back bumper. He said he had no idea. Then I asked him who installed it, and with a smile he thumped his chest, and I understood why. As it turns out, Angel spent a great portion of his time standing on that bumper hanging on for dear life as he directed the driver in the way he should go. I reasoned that if I spent my time standing on the back bumper of a Jeep as it threatened to go supersonic, I would want to be sure the bumper was secure myself, as well.

Personally, I was glad to hear of the quality installation. You see, one of my chief pleasures in life while working in Cali was to stand on that same bumper and hang on for dear life as we careened up and down the mountain.

Years ago Christian, that year's driver, held Angel's position, and he and I struck up a friendship in the same way Angel and I had. One morning a few years back, as we left the city behind and began the dirt road climb up the mountain, Christian tapped me on the shoulder and invited me to share the bumper with him. It was a moment of acceptance and a bit of a test, I believe. So I gladly stepped out into the morning sunshine, and I have refused to relinquish my position from that time to this.

A peaceful freedom overtook me when I stepped out onto that bumper that was truly wonderful. The shackles of fear seemed to fall away, and my spirit relaxed within me as my muscles tightened their grip. When I felt the wind on my face, I began to see the world anew. There is no use in me trying to explain it, as it must be experienced. It is an awakening of sorts.

This past year, the bumper didn't beckon; the rear seat of a rickety and ramshackle motorbike did as we left Brisis Del Mar and headed for the coast.

The motorbike was of the same manufacturer as the Jeep, the driver projected the same mixture of peaceful insanity as did Angel and Christian, and the ride was a bit more challenging than the mountain, if that is possible. As I tumbled down the hillside with the bike more airborne than earthbound, that same odd since of freedom and peace overtook me again, so I decided to examine it.

Where does it come from? Why is it there? It occurred to me that perhaps this particular brand of freedom, this particular brand of spiritual peace, can only be obtained when we step out of bounds a little.

Most of us spend our Christian life in a carefully ordered spiritual vacuum of sorts. We are often afraid to color outside of the lines. We live out our Christianity as if we are painting by numbers in fear that should the yellow bleed over into the red, disaster will follow.

Well, I contend that if God can make Eden out of chaos, joy out of sorrow, and eternal life out of death, then He can make a blessing out of anything done in His name.

It seems to me that true blessings seldom occur in a carefully planned, sterile environment. God seems to love to work in haphazard and surprising ways. So let the colors run a bit in your life. Relax and bask in the freedom Christ gives you. Find blessings in all things.

Step out onto the bumper of life, careen down a hill or two, cast off your fear of the unknown, and know God is always before you, always behind you, and always with you, yearning to bless you.

Colombia Cutie, Cali, Colombia, by Tony Rowell

Trespassers Will Be Fed to the Hogs

"Didn't you see the signs, son? What are you doing in my yard?"

"What sign?" I stammered.

He was 250 pounds if he was an ounce, and he didn't look particularly thrilled at my being there.

"The sign that says, 'Trespassers will be fed to the hogs.'"

He paused to let that sink in. His face gave a little spasm that lifted his upper lip just enough to hint at the yellowish and brown teeth behind the veil.

"THAT SIGN," he said.

"Well, no sir, augh, ah, I didn't. I truly apologize, but I didn't see it."

"Then you're either blind or stupid. Considering you're down this trail this late in the day all by your little lonesome, I would guess stupid."

I had been hiking down the River Trail in the Congaree National Park for four hours or so. The River Trail is the lengthiest trail the park has to offer, and on account of that, it is seldom used.

Most folks consider one mile or less a walk and everything beyond that a hike. Hikers consider anything under five miles to be a walk and everything beyond that to be a hike.

The River Trail comes in at about eleven and a half miles, and since most visitors to the park either don't have the time necessary to make the trek or the wherewithal to handle it, it is a wonderful hike for those who hunger after solitude. I fall into that category, and I hike on account of that condition.

To the best of my recollection, it was either late July or early August several years back. It may have been a bit later. On second thought it was. It was during "Indian Summer." You know, the latter days of August or sometimes just when September starts. Those cool autumn breezes have winked at you but not settled in yet, and then in a last-ditch effort to assert itself, summer summons up one last hot breath that startles and stifles the world.

It was at that time that I was working my way down the trail. It was wonderfully quiet that day. Even the dragonflies and mosquitoes considered flight too much of an effort in the heat. There was a slight breeze, but other than that, the world was at rest, and I was in hog heaven.

You see, I spent most all of my summers down on the panhandle of Florida with my grandparents when I was a kid, and the panhandle is perpetually in an "Indian Summer" state. So I wasn't hot that afternoon. I was a young'un again.

I suppose that may have been one of the reasons I wasn't paying particularly close attention. I had been hiking for a while like I said, oh, maybe six and a half, seven miles before I noticed anything askew.

Now, the floor of the Congaree Swamp is made up of whatever Mother Nature chooses to put there, and Mother Nature isn't always one to keep a clean house. Basically, the floor of the Congaree Swamp is a wild chaos of disorderly fallen limbs, downed trees, and cypress knees, along with a wonderful assortment of roots running every which-a-way.

What I had failed to notice as I wandered through the woods dreaming of days gone by were the occasional patches of orderly chaos hidden within the regular, run of the mill chaos of the swamp.

Here and there, it was kind of like somebody was looking for something. Occasionally there was dirt pushed up and scattered around with the limbs and leaves pushed to the side. Now, I knew no one had done it. After all, considering its condition, I had little doubt that I was the only person who had been down that particular trail for a long while.

The truth is I actually knew what it was, but I wasn't concerned. These little patches are all over the swamp, so I paid little attention.

The increase in size and frequency was gradual, so gradual in fact that I failed to notice it until, when rounding a blind curve, a slight whiff of musk hit my nostrils a millisecond before that primordial sound hit my ears.

If you have never heard a full-grown razorback hog with malice on his mind say grace before his evening meal ten feet from your face, then I pray you never do.

I still find it amazing, but with a herculean effort I managed to keep my wits about me and remain relatively continent at the same time. At least I didn't scream like a little girl, pick up my skirts, and run back down the trail willy-nilly.

Somehow I knew that to do so would be considered rude by the hog, and with feelings hurt, he would chase me down and kill me without a second thought or the slightest twinge of guilt. So I stood my ground, weak knees and all.

Razorback hogs don't look like regular eating hogs. They look like hogs from the wrong side of the tracks. Hogs you don't want to mess with. They've got little beady eyes, spiked hair, switchblade tusks, black leather jackets with studs, and an attitude to match the outfit.

Now, I had a .22 caliber pistol with me for protection, against what I don't know. Instinctively, however, I knew that to shoot this hog before me with a .22 caliber pistol would act more as an inspiration to him than a deterrent, so I chose the middle ground and shot a tree. That hog didn't even flinch. Actually, he looked more insulted than startled.

After that, he looked me over a couple of times, decided I was more bone and gristle than meat and not even worth the effort. So he turned away, disgusted, and sauntered back down the trail the way he had come, grumbling under his breath the whole time.

After he was out of sight and his grumblings had faded, I discovered that remaining upright was not an option for me at that moment. So I decided it might be a good time to sit down and rest for a spell. For a long, long spell.

The world and the sin it traffics in can sneak up on you if you're not paying close attention. The changes are often gradual, barely noticeable most of the time. A little compromise here, a small compromise there, and then one day you round a blind curve, and there it is: a compromised life, a witness diminished, a faith in crisis.

So remember to keep your eyes on Christ and Christ alone. He will keep you from falling prey to the world. He will protect your faith, strengthen your witness, and make your life more wonderful, more joyous than you could have ever imagined without Him.

Grits

One morning a while back, I was sitting in a hotel room down in Atlanta. For the life of me, I can't remember why I was there, but I do remember the moment when I began to sense my cholesterol was running a bit low. It also hit me about the same time that I was beginning to feel a little like the Tin Man right before he ran out of machine oil. Everything creaked and cracked and hurt like the devil. John Denver wrote in one of his songs that "time whispers when it's cold." That may have been true for him, but time was cutting loose in full voice this morning, letting me know the foolishness of my younger days was catching up with me in a hurry.

When this happens, as it often does, I usually search around for a suitable remedy to the problem. On this particular morning I was in luck, for less than a half a mile down the road rested none other than that icon of the American way of life (and eating, I might add): Waffle House.

I figured I could increase my cholesterol and grease my joints at the same time, so I took a walk on the wild side and braved the mean streets of Atlanta. I headed for that dirty yellow sign with the big black letters.

I walked in, received the mandatory "How are you this morning?" from a face that showed no interest whatsoever, sat down, and ordered two over well, with grits and bacon. Along with that I ordered a cup of the most consistently bad coffee on the planet. I was in paradise. I just love Waffle House. If you like people and good food, and aren't particular about who you hang around with or how your food is prepared, then Waffle House is the place for you.

I have always contended that had the stable been located in Waycross, Georgia, instead of Bethlehem and had Jesus been raised in the Southern U.S. instead of the Middle East, Waffle House would have been one of His favorite haunts. You see, Christ loved the folks, and He wasn't particular about who He hung around with—and nobody can resist two over well with grits and bacon.

Now if you really want to have some fun, find a Waffle House near an airport or an interstate. Not an even-numbered interstate, mind you, but an odd-numbered one, say I-95—one that heads south to north (or north to south, if you've got good sense). Once you've settled in and ordered, all you have to do is just sit and wait. You're fishing. What you're fishing for is an accent that leaves no doubt whatsoever that whoever the owner of that accent might be: "ain't from round here." New York will do in a pinch, but second only to New Hampshire; Massachusetts wears the crown—a Boston, Massachusetts, accent in particular.

Once your quarry has been located and hopefully settled into the booth next to yours, pray with all your might for two things. First of all, pray your new friends have never enjoyed the culinary delights of grits. Secondly, pray they have enough courage and curiosity to take a leap of faith and order two over well, with grits and bacon. As a side note, also pray there is no ketchup within a twenty-five-mile radius of your location, because if there is, just as sure as God made little green apples, they'll cover their grits with it and ruin all the fun.

Once the waitress brings their order and answers all their questions—and there will be many—and after they have checked with Google to see what side effects grit ingestion might cause, all you have to do is sit still and listen and try to maintain your composure. I promise you: You will have the time of your life.

I considered trying to reconstruct some of the conversations I have heard over the years from adjacent booths, but try as I might I simply could not do them justice. I suppose you just have to be there. I know this, though: When listening to your neighbors discuss the attributes of grits, be cautious while drinking your coffee. Consistently bad or not, that stuff burns like the dickens when an ill-timed chuckle sends it upstream.

So what deep sociological or inspired theological lesson can be found in this story? None whatsoever, that I can see. I suppose I could talk about the strength of grits as opposed to the weakness of a grit, but that might come across as a little contrived.

The truth is, I figured we could all use a little break. Between the angst on the news, the tension in our denomination, and life in general, a story about nothing in particular with no deep and lasting meaning sounded kind of appealing to me.

So rest your mind, calm your heart, enjoy your grits, and know that God's got this, whatever this might be.

The Destination

I keep an old television with a DVD player attached to it down in my workshop to keep me company. As a rule, I stick a movie in there or a Hogan's Heroes, and once in a while, I'll put an old Andy Griffith in and listen to Barney rant and rave. Well, the other day, I was down in the shop working on this and that, and I put an Andy in. As I watched the opening credits with Opie and Andy walking down that old dirt road chucking rocks in the lake, my mind went nostalgic, as it often does, and it hit me that that was my life during the summers when I was a kid.

I am a contemporary of Opie, you see. Old Ron Howard and I are close in age, so in actuality, when I was a kid, my life was not all that different from Opie's.

During the summer months when I was with Granny and Grandpa, I walked those old southern dirt roads down on the Florida Panhandle, kicking cans, chucking rocks, and getting into all sorts of mischief.

I fished whenever I could and played whenever I couldn't, and in the evenings, if a ball game wasn't on, I would sit on the old front porch and occupy myself somehow. Yes, there was life before video games and satellite television.

Sometimes I would just go out on the carport and sit silently beside my grandpa finding comfort in the glow of his Pall Mall cigarette. Listening to the night sounds and watching the toads make their way to the cool concrete for the night, I was content and at peace.

I slept on the old front porch throughout the summer. It had jalousie windows, for those who know what I'm talking about, and the bed was a door, laid flat, with makeshift legs and a bit of cushion on it. Hard as a stone, but familiar, so I rested easy on it.

I would lie out there on Thursday nights and listen to Dragnet. You see, Granny's next door neighbor, Irene, was hard of hearing, and she kept her TV loud and her windows open. So when I heard, "Just the facts, ma'am," I would sit up and enjoy the show. It was a treat.

On Sunday afternoons, we went visiting. We would take off to Cottondale, Chipley, or Crestview to visit great aunts and uncles; first, second and third cousins; and old friends.

Being a child, I hated it then, but I miss it now. I miss it now that life has gotten so busy that visiting is out of style, that just dropping by to say "hi" is an imposition instead of a pleasure, that sitting on the front porch in the cool of the day can't seem to be tolerated by many folks anymore without some electronic gadget in their hands to distract them.

I know I am sounding old, a little crotchety, and way too nostalgic, and perhaps that is the case. But I miss the days when life was gradual and relationships, real relationships, were cherished. To quote Merle Haggard, I kinda long for the days when "Coke was still cola and a joint was a bad place to be."

When I was a bit younger, I would not have understood what I have just written. At that time, I was in the midst of life, with children to raise, a career to tend to, schedules to keep and adventures to take. I would have never understood, had I told myself then, that running through life at a hundred miles an hour doesn't augment life; it diminishes it.

A laser focus may get you to where you want to be, only to have you discover that you left what truly matters behind. Remember, a hollow victory is no victory at all.

As your friend, please slow down long enough to experience the life God has given you. Don't let your life be a blur on the side of the road. Enjoy it.

Take the time to love those God has given you to love. Take the time to be loved.

Life is so much more than getting to a destination. Life is the destination.

So slow down a bit and enjoy the ride.

Bolivian Daydream, by Tony Rowell

Letting It Fly

I awoke to the sound of a blue jay squawking just outside the window, and for once I didn't mind all that much. Mary and I were down at the beach enjoying a wonderful time of peace and restful slumber, and the sound of the jay seemed right.

Later that morning as we walked down to the beach, just a block away, the smell of salt mist on the air, the far-off cries of a couple of seagulls, and the distinctive crackle of live oak leaves underfoot began to awaken some well-worn memories of mine.

It wasn't long until I was a barefoot boy down in Panama City, Florida, again listening to the blue jays up in the chinaberry trees and seeking out the perfect stone for the slingshot in my hand.

My Granny Tharpe was a lover of all living things. I suppose it was the Creek Indian in her, but other than any eating-size fish, she tended to live and let live. The one exception to the rule was blue jays. I don't know how it happened, but apparently in her youth a blue jay had really hurt her feelings, and being well practiced in the art of revenge, she had been on a seek-and-destroy mission ever since. My brother, Mike, and I had been recruited into her private army and given permission to harass the blue jay population by any and all means possible.

On this particular summer afternoon, my weapon of choice—well, actually the only weapon Granny would let a six-year-old have—was an old handmade slingshot. With a properly forked branch, a couple of strips of inner tube, and a piece of old shoe leather, I had fashioned what I fancied to be a precision instrument of destruction.

I listened carefully to determine the location of my quarry, and to my delight, just ten feet above me and a little to the left, sat a big fat blue jay on one of the lower limbs of the catawba tree in Granny's backyard.

I had the perfect stone. Not too big, not too little, and as smooth as can be. Just the right weight, you know, with enough heft to do the job and yet light enough to maintain its speed and trajectory once released.

As the sun began to set in the west, I licked my right index finger, lifted it into the air, and determined wind speed and direction. I adjusted for humidity and distance. When all was set, I squinted against the setting sun's glare, sighted-in on my target, and let fly.

Upon my release, sensing the danger, the jay leapt into the air and, in so doing, relieved the branch of its burden. In response the branch rose up, only an inch or so, but just enough to redirect my projectile. In disbelief and rising horror I watched, as if in slow motion, as the stone headed for and crashed through the only window available for miles, it seemed.

Upon entering Granny's utility room, the stone ricocheted about, and in so doing, found its true calling. It dented Granny's brand-new washer door, played havoc with several fishing rods and reels, took out a couple of jars of home-canned tomatoes, and finally came to rest inside an old cricket box.

I have to give her this much. Granny was fast. Before the echo faded, Granny was advancing on me at a rapid pace with something akin to hellfire in her eyes, her own precision instrument of destruction held fast in her right hand.

I think it was the combination of disappointment, utter astonishment, and sheer horror in my eyes that stopped her progress. It didn't take her long to assess the situation, and as the grin swept across her face, followed by her signature cackle, I knew I would survive to fight another day.

She looked down at me and asked if I had gotten him, but there was no need to answer, for that blue jay was sitting on an upper limb looking down and laughing for all he was worth.

Late in the afternoon all those years ago, I learned a couple of things that have held me in good stead over the years. First and foremost, mercy is a wonderful thing to receive, and in turn, I have tried to be as merciful over the years as my Granny was that summer's evening. Secondly, I learned all things must be considered before I let anything fly.

I have to admit it is that last lesson that I tend to forget, especially when it comes to my words. How about you?

Surrender

The first time I ever set foot on an airplane was way back in 1972. My Grandfather Rowell had passed away, and since Dad, with my brother and sister in tow, had driven down earlier, Mom and I boarded a Southern Airways Martin 404 at the Columbia airport for the trip down to Panama City. We went to gather with the family to celebrate the life of a man of whom I knew little, but for whom I held a great deal of love, nonetheless.

I will leave the story of Grandpa Rowell for another day. For now, let me tell you about the flight.

For those uninitiated, the Martin 404 was an old forty-passenger two-engine prop plane. It was quite noisy with the propellers spinning away on both wings and you in the middle, and to say the flight was smooth would be to lie. Actually, it ranged somewhere between a flat tire and rollercoaster most of the time, but it got you there, as a rule.

On this particular day, the thunderstorms of the South were apparently having a family reunion, because from Columbia to Panama City we did nothing but dodge the things. Make that, we dodged most of them. I was thrilled at the time, though. You see, I love a rollercoaster, and to my young mind, it was a great ride.

All of that changed somewhere over Tifton, Georgia, to the best of my recollection. For it was there that the plane, having zigged when it should have zagged, skipped over the top of a thunderhead and proceeded to drop like a stone over the other side. As we sped toward the red clay of Georgia at breakneck speed, it suddenly dawned on me that I had no control—none whatsoever. I had foolishly listened to my mother and handed the reins of my life over to some guy I had never met sitting in the nose of the plane. I didn't know his name, his background, nothing, and yet my entire future depended upon what he did in the next few minutes. Boy, did I feel dumb or what?

In retrospect, though, it appears to me that Southern Airways had a policy of hiring former fighter pilots because with the strength of Samson and the skill of Chuck Yeager, our pilot regained control of the plane. Quickly thereafter, he left our stomachs at about three thousand feet and popped that old plane back up to the top of the clouds just like a cork. I have loved flying ever since.

Galatians 2:20 reads as follows: "I have been crucified with Christ and I no longer live, but Christ lives in me."

To my mind, those words mean that in order for me to truly follow Christ, I must voluntarily surrender my independence into the hands of Christ, just as I unwittingly surrendered my life into the hands of that pilot all those years ago. In so doing, I surrender my say-so to Christ so that His say-so can rule in my life.

The key word here is voluntarily. No one else can hand over the reins of my life to Christ, except me. Christ is not going to wrest them from my grasp. Christ is no tyrant. Christ is a gentle, loving God who is not looking to conquer me, but to have me join Him in His ministry to the world.

In order for this to take place in my life, I must be willing to shed the independence I so prize and totally yield to the supremacy of my Lord Jesus Christ. I must no longer live for my own ideas, for my own wants, for my own agenda. I must live totally for Christ.

Complete loyalty to Christ is what is needed if I truly want my life to be used for the Kingdom of God. Without such loyalty, without the release of my independence, my life—while appearing for all the world to be lived for Christ—will in truth be nothing more than a pious charade. I may appear to be a man of God, but in truth, without surrendering my independence to Christ, I will be nothing but a fraud.

The question I must ask myself is this: "Am I willing to give it all to Christ? Am I willing to hand over all of my dreams, all of my aspirations, all of my everything so that I may be used by Christ in whatever fashion He chooses? Am I willing to be 'crucified with Christ?' Am I willing to have Christ help Himself to me?"

On a more personal level, are you willing to let go of everything for Christ? Are you willing to let Christ help Himself to your agenda, your wants, and your desires? Are you willing to allow Christ to help himself to whatever He needs, no matter what?

Are you, like Paul before you, willing to "consider them rubbish, that you may gain Christ and be found in him" (Philippians 3:8-9)?

I pray you are willing. For Christ needs men and women of the cross, duly crucified with Him, to carry His message of forgiveness and salvation to a world desperately seeking His touch.

Tom

I suppose John Steinbeck was right. Some stories can't be told; they must be cajoled and teased into existence. To force the issue only tatters the wings and takes away the magic.

Yarns are like moths and butterflies that way. Let a little boy reach out to satisfy his curiosity, let him touch a wing ever so gently, and that mystical, magical covering of dust is troubled—and that luckless moth will forever be earthbound from that ill-fated point on.

To examine a moth, one must induce it to crawl up on a leaf, knife blade, or finger to be carried to the eye. The delicacy of the creature demands a gentle touch. To do otherwise is to destroy it, and that, my friend, is a sin. Stories, like moths, take a bit of coaxing from time to time.

Many years ago, I was a custom cabinetmaker, and my workshop was housed in a picturesque old two-story barn just up the hill from my home. I built my shop on the lower level. I wired it and walled it, but I left the old heart pine floor alone, chiefly because the gaps between the boards cut down on sweeping and the accumulated sawdust underneath provided nice bedding for the myriad critters that shared the barn with me.

Every morning I was greeted by my menagerie, not with squeaks or howls, but with a fusion of wild, exotic, and somewhat organic odors. Rats and snakes, bats and squirrels, and a host of creepy crawlies sought shelter and comfort in that old barn, as did I. I loved being there.

Inside the shop up against the wall was an old staircase that gave way to the upstairs. At the top of the thing was a small opening, just big enough to walk through if you ducked. I closed it off during the winter to stave off freezing, but in the summer I opened it up to enjoy the cross breeze and air out the place. Romantic or not, South Carolina heat and the leavings of a menagerie do not make good companions.

One late summer's afternoon, I was working on a raised panel or something of that sort over at the bench when I began to feel as if I was being watched. My instinct drew my eyes to the top of the stairs, where an adolescent cat sat placidly giving me the once-over.

The thing looked like a gang member: wiry, distrustful, and dangerous. He was mostly white with a few gang tats, one over his left eye, one on his right foot, and the final one on the very tip of his tail, all done in prison black. He was wearing a "Well, Buddy, I suppose we have to share this barn, but don't mess with me, 'cause I don't like being trifled with" expression.

When our eyes met, he didn't flinch or twitch or bolt, as most feral creatures would. He held contact for a second or two, yawned luxuriously, as if to remind me I was beneath his contempt, and then rising, he ever so slowly sauntered off.

His is a story I cannot tell. It took me a year or two just to get him to stop looking at me like that, and try as I may, no matter how much I coaxed or flattered, and no matter what delicacies or delights I placed before him, that little cat shared that barn with me for years and always managed to maintain his sovereignty and distinctly haughty air.

Now, while I would be hard-pressed to tell his story without an excess of augmentation, I can tell you of Tom.

Tom is a Latvian cat. Well, actually he is just a little kitten, prepubescent at most. In any case, he is young enough and innocent enough to trust without question the Americans who come to visit his home country and invade his privacy and his lodgings. Tom is the house cat of the hotel Pie Jāņa Brāļa, where my United Methodist Volunteers in Mission team was housed in Liepaja, Latvia, during the two weeks we remained in that beautiful and peace-filled place. I will expand upon that wonderful country later, but for now, let's stick to Tom.

Tom is the polar opposite of his barn-dwelling counterpart. Tom is everybody's friend. He carries with him an air of love and acceptance. His default position in life is one of peace toward and empathy for all creatures, no matter their origin or attitude.

Like my friend from years past, Tom's coat is based in white, but carries within it a smattering of various gray hues and just a hint of brown, or rather sandstone. In spite of a pair of eyes that are set just a bit too far apart, giving him a slightly confused expression, he is a pretty cat—or rather a handsome cat. No, I will stick with pretty, as that better describes him. Or rather, her.

You see, Tom is a conflicted cat. He was given the name "Tom" by a passing child when he first arrived at the hotel. It wasn't until after the name stuck that anyone took the time to discover his true gender, which as it turns out is female. By the time of the discovery, Tom was Tom, and no girly name would fit her. So Tom it is.

Tom is a people cat, and at first I thought Tom was an indiscriminate, flighty people-cat jumping on any knee that would have her, but as it turned out she was just testing the waters. She was searching out a harbor, a place where she could rest safe and secure, and she found her resting place on John's knee. Cats know cat people.

Every morning during breakfast, she would cruise up and down the tables until she found John, then she would jump up on his knee, curl up in a tight little ball, and drift off to sleep while he gently stroked her from head to tail. She knew she was safe there. She knew she was accepted there. She did try to step out of bounds and steal a tidbit or two from time to time, but with one quiet word from John, she would put her head back down and return to sleep.

Late at night I would wander down to the dining room, sit on the couch there, and play an old guitar to soothe nerves. When Tom heard the first note, she climbed up on the back of the couch and, using my left shoulder as a step, jumped down onto the guitar, settled into the hollow and purred herself to sleep. But I played second fiddle to John. He was her favorite. She only had eyes for him when he could be found.

At first, I wondered what the Lord was up to in coaxing this story from me. To be honest, from moths and butterflies to feral cats and knees, it was a bit of a mystery. Interesting enough, I suppose, but what's the message?

As I was finishing my writing, the simplicity of the message became clear. In this troubled world, there are times when a child of God and the church of God simply need to be a safe harbor for those seeking shelter. There is a time to offer rest and rest alone from a world gone mad. There is a time when all that is needed is a loving embrace and a place where the lost, be they barn- or knee-dwellers, can feel safe enough to just curl up and rest.

Of course, the Word of God must be preached or the lost will never find their true home, but they cannot listen without rest.

The Holy Scriptures declare rest is not a thing we do, but rather a place where we reside. Let us be that place for the lost, for the troubled, and for those living in fear. Let us—as the children and the church of the Most High—be a place of peace and rest.

The Weather Vane

I can still hear that high-pitched screeching as it spun overhead.

I was in my Great Aunt Mary's old general store in Cottondale, Florida. It was a Sunday afternoon in early summer, and Granny and Grandpa and I were visiting family again, like it or not.

Aunt Mary was my Grandpa Tharpe's oldest sister. She had basically raised Grandpa, what with his momma and daddy both dying early in his life. She was the quietest of his three sisters, and the most reclusive. Why a recluse opens up a general store I'll never know, but she did.

She was a classic spinster—never married, greatly revered in town, and she carried with her the proud air of settled loneliness.

I can't say I knew her very well; she didn't allow me to. I don't think she cared for children all that much. But I sure did love being in her calming presence, and I loved her old store.

It was all closed up by the time I came around, but she never cleaned it out. What was there on the day she closed the doors for the last time stayed, and I don't think she ever went back in.

She would let me and my brother plunder in there from time to time, as a way to get us out from underfoot, but other than that, I don't think she ever darkened the door.

Well, on this particular day, I was plundering on my own. Mike had gone back to Utica with the family a week or so before, which left me to take care of the mischievousness all by myself. I was well versed in the art, and possessed a tendency toward mischief that was the envy of many of my contemporaries, so the duty wasn't a burden.

I was in there looking for trouble and snakeskins—we called them scalps back then—and was doing pretty well for myself when that screeching started. It filled the room with the most awfulest of sounds. It sounded like a thousand fingernails on a chalkboard with just a hint of Rosanne Barr's voice mixed in. It was dreadful.

Well, I had to get out of there or go crazy, so I ran out to the front yard. Then I looked back, trying to figure out where that horrible sound was coming from, and it didn't take me long to figure it out.

The old weather vane, complete with a galvanized tin arrow and a rooster on top, was spinning like a dreidel and shrieking like a demon. It just couldn't decide which way to go.

I was so focused on its spinning and that wicked sound it made that I failed to notice the blackness behind it and the wind in my ears. Then all of a sudden, the thing made up its mind, and there I was with the arrow pointed straight at me and the rooster wondering what I was doing standing around when I ought to be high-tailing it out of there.

Well, I decided that rooster had a point. That ghastly sound was preferable to whatever was hiding behind that blackness, so I headed back into the building, hands over my ears with my stomach in my throat. About that time the storm hit—howling wind first, followed by a driving rain, a frog strangler as Granny would say, and then a hailstorm like none before or since.

I have always loved the sound of a gentle rain on a tin roof; that sound will lull you to sleep in a skinny minute. But hail is another thing altogether. I thought it was going to drive my scrawny little frame into the ground like a railroad spike, but God is good, and I was only ankle-deep when the commotion stopped just as quickly as it started.

As it turns out, the storm took out a bunch of trees and a couple of houses on the other side of town, but the only thing missing from Aunt Mary's place was the aforementioned weather vane. Never saw it again. It's either in orbit, or it's over near Chipley. One way or the other, the screeching stopped.

My young mind had been fascinated by weather vanes up until then. Before that day, I looked at them as toys. You know, something you threw rocks at and made spin when boredom overtook you. I thought they were really neat, but I never looked at them as tools.

I learned that day that weather vanes will tell you what's coming. They will warn you of danger if you are paying attention—and you'd better be paying attention.

Lately some in the church have been throwing rocks at the weather vane trying to make it turn in a way that suits their fancy. Some prefer a gentle horizontal breeze to a stiff vertical one; it's just more pleasant. It's easier to deal with. That gentle breeze doesn't ruffle nearly as many feathers as the stiff one does. Oh, that stiff breeze may expose the chaff and clean things up a bit making it suitable, but who wants that? That only makes for work.

So they keep throwing their irreverent rocks, hoping against hope that the keeper of the wind will relent, but they are tilting at windmills. That is an ancient wind, and it has been challenged time and time again never to yield, forever standing firm.

We had best be very careful as a people and as a church lest, in our arrogance and pride, we lose our direction and find ourselves carried away by the winds.

The Holy Scriptures are not of our making. We would be well advised to remember that!

Matthew 5:18, "For truly I tell you, until heaven and earth disappear, not the smallest letter, not the least stroke of a pen, will by any means disappear from the Law until everything is accomplished" (NIV).

The Road Seldom Traveled

I know I am not alone in my concern for the church of Christ, its people, and its purpose. It seems to me that the world is making inroads into the Body of Christ at breakneck speed, as of late. I could describe what's been going on, but there is no need. Even those who agree with the changes will have to admit Christian norms are being challenged on a daily basis.

I'm not talking about the hot-button topics of human sexuality and the like exclusively, either. I am talking about the popular notion that the truths of God are no longer concrete, but rather fluid and changing, the idea that to speak of morality and following "The Way" is passé. I am speaking of the fact that, in many minds, social justice trumps the Holy Scriptures.

I am not a militant by any means, but I am concerned that many within the body are constructing their theologies upon a shifting foundation. The societal pendulum swings to and fro continually, and to attach any permanence to it seems questionable, at a minimum.

I fear the attempt to demonstrate the love of Christ, no matter the circumstance, by declaring that "all is well, Christ will forgive"—or the more concerning parsing of God's word to suit the situation at hand—is testing the forbearance of our Creator. Yes, of course Christ will forgive, provided we accept His definition of right and wrong and then confess, and repent of the wrongdoing. I love the verse from the book of Job, "Submit to God, and you will have peace; then things will go well for you" (22:21 NLT).

To declare the Holy Scriptures must play second-fiddle to the whims of society simply because we disagree with what is written in them is a dangerous road upon which to travel.

There, I have said my piece, and I know many disagree with me, and that is fine. I am not here to judge; that's God's job.

Years ago, when the winds were beginning to change and I had no idea the Lord was planning on calling me to the pulpit ministry, I was pulling corn on my quarter-acre plot near Gilbert. While doing so, I absentmindedly pondered the changes taking place at the time and the coming changes that concerned me, and a poem came to mind. I would like to share it with you.

It is titled "The Road Seldom Traveled," and it speaks of a narrow lane—the narrow lane of following Christ no matter what winds or currents we may face in life

The Road Seldom Traveled

Have you ever seen a byway that's been alone too long,
with ruts that cut so deep, and weeds that grow so long?
The trees they overhang it, with shadows all around,
and you wonder, "Should I bother, or head on back to town?"

For that road is narrow, dark and long, with stones upon the ground,
and my feet are very tender, and a smooth way can't be found.
For I haven't had a chance you see, to toughen up my soles,
against the stones upon the ground or the thorns the weeds may hold.

'Sides, that road is seldom traveled, and then only by a few.
Who say they met a man along the way to help them through.
They said His name was Jesus, and a strange thing I was told.
He gave them all he had for free. Not a thing was sold.

Now this road that I've been travelin' down is wide and often trod,
by folks somewhat like me, in search of a lesser god.
A god who won't require restraint, or ask us to obey;
we want a god to save our souls, for something we can pay.

"I'd like two pounds of Jesus please, not enough to weigh me down,
just enough to help me make it through, till I reach another town.
Any less of Him won't fill the void; any more might make a change.
And I like my life the way it is. I don't want to rearrange."

Strange.

So we travel down our roads in life with hope that at the end,
the little bits of good we do will counteract the sin.
But we could work both day and night, with all the work in vain.

For the only way to reach the light,
is down that narrow lane.

"Enter through the narrow gate. For wide is the gate and broad is the road that leads to destruction, and many enter through it. But small is the gate and narrow the road that leads to life, and only a few find it" (Matthew 7:13-14 NIV).

"Therefore Jesus said again, 'Very truly I tell you, I am the gate for the sheep. All who have come before me are thieves and robbers, but the sheep have not listened to them. I am the gate; whoever enters through me will be saved. They will come in and go out, and find pasture'" (John 10:7-9 NIV).

Give It Up

Some of you might not know this, but from the seventh grade all the way through my senior year in high school, I didn't live with my parents. Make that, I didn't sleep in the same place as they did. I slept in a mobile home right next to theirs with my brother, Mike. That's right. I had a bachelor pad from an early age.

You see, a 12x64-foot mobile home gets a bit tight with three kids in it, and since second stories don't work well with mobile homes, Mom and Dad simply found an old trailer and set Mike and me up in it. We had twenty acres a few miles outside of Lexington, so there was plenty of room. It was a great solution to the overcrowding problem.

Mike had the bedroom on the far end, and I had the one closest to Mom and Dad. Apparently, I was the less trustworthy of the two. Mike and I set up a music studio of sorts in the middle. It was great. I bet you wish you'd been so lucky as a kid.

We lived way out in the woods at that time. We had all sorts of critters around to make it interesting for a young boy, and lots of creepy crawlies to scare the girls. While we were by no means the Clampetts, we raised chickens and goats, we had a couple of horses and the like, and in my opinion such a life is to be envied.

Unfortunately, over the years civilization has encroached and lots of the critters have left for more suitable lodgings, but the owls and an occasional coon still give the place a wonderful woodsy air.

It did have its disadvantages, though. When you live in the woods, your property is not strictly your own; the creepy crawlies tend to stake a claim to your home, as well. I discovered that one night at about 2 a.m. when I was awakened by a scorpion who was offended that I had invaded his space without an invitation. The problem was that I had staked a claim on my bed years before. Nonetheless, he registered his disapproval by stinging me right in the middle of the bottom of my left foot. He accomplished what he intended. I left, and I left quickly.

I used to love hearing my mother tell the story of the next day. She could never get all the way through the story without ending up in that breathless laugh of hers that I so loved to hear.

I was in a rage at the time, so my memory is clouded a bit; but Mom claimed that the next day, I spent several hours hobbling around scouring all twenty acres, looking under every rock I could find collecting the kinfolks of the offending scorpion. I placed them all in a pot I had gotten from the kitchen, added a touch of gasoline for flavor, and sent them all home.

The part Mom truly loved to tell, though, was what happened the day after the great scorpion immolation, when I was confronted with yet another scorpion as he sat on the kitchen linoleum and pondered the Grim Reaper before him. Mom used to tell me the look I had of fear mixed with astonishment, utter disappointment, and impotent rage was priceless—just before I threw up my hands and walked out.

I learned a valuable lesson back then that has been reinforced time and time again as the years have gone by. Namely, that trouble is going to come in this life, and the second you think you have it handled, it will pick a new angle and come at you again.

So the question isn't, "Will troubles come?" Rather it is, "When troubles come, what are we going to do about it?"

Now in that this is being written by a preacher, I bet you already know the answer I am seeking. That being said, knowing the answer and acting on that answer are two separate things altogether. So I suppose my ultimate question is, "When troubles come your way, are you actually planning to give them to Christ right from the beginning, or would you rather engage in that fruitless struggle we are all so familiar with first, and then give them to Christ?"

As difficult as I know it can be sometimes, I would suggest you simply hand the problems over to Christ right from the beginning and enjoy the rest only Christ can give even in the midst of troubles.

As many of us can attest, troubles will come in this life when we least expect them, but Christ is always there as expected. Lean on Him when times get difficult. Give Him your burdens. He does so long to share them with you. Never forget that when Christ said, "Come to Me, all you who labor and are heavy laden, and I will give you rest" (Matthew 11:28), He truly meant it.

One Wild Ride

Let me tell you about one of the most exciting days of my life. It happened years ago in Manila, Philippines. It was my first mission trip, my first time overseas, and the first time of many that I came close to wetting my pants in public.

I can tell you this: I was in for some surprises and a host of other things of which I could have never dreamed. Aside from the totally different culture with its different customs, not to mention different people; there were odd foods to be tried and natural sights that boggled the mind. Over and above all of that, there were some things that we new missionaries would be asked to do for which we were ill-prepared.

I, at the time, was a building contractor, and that is what I knew. I knew how to build things. That is what I had come to the Philippines to do. I was bound and determined to build a church for God. I was very well prepared to do that. I looked forward to doing that. That was my thing, after all.

But upon arriving in Manila, it appeared the folks in charge had something else planned first. They actually wanted us to go out to different churches and talk. I mean talk, instead of the preacher. I was horrified. I didn't talk in public. The only way I would get up in front of a crowd was with a guitar in front of me to hide behind, and Mary had to do all the talking, and even then I was scared to death most of the time. I thought to myself, "When does the next plane leave for home? I have had enough of this pie already, thank you."

The worst part about the whole thing is we had arrived on a Saturday night and the nuts wanted us to talk the next morning. I just about cried.

Well, needless to say, I didn't like it very much, but I did it. As it turned out though, that Sunday morning was a big turning-point in my life as a man and a Christian.

I had no choice, it seemed, so I accepted my sentence, prayed for the poor congregation I was being foisted upon and waited for the preacher to pick me up, praying for engine failure the whole time.

Have you ever noticed how the Lord picks on those He loves? Well if that's the case, then I feel sure He loves me half to death because He sure got me that morning.

I was close to the youngest and by far the most nervous of the lot, so I was naturally the last one picked up. Oh, I forgot to tell you—we had to go alone, with no one from the team with us.

Well, finally a brand-new Jeep Renegade drove up and a fine-looking young man about my age jumped out, shook my hand, and we were off. I said to myself, "Maybe I was wrong. This might not be so bad." We drove thirty miles or so to the other side of Manila and finally ended up on an island named Muzon at the little Muzon United Methodist Church where I was to speak.

I won't go into the service, other than to say the Lord will save you if you cry and beg enough. The preacher, Ben Azurin, happened to have a guitar, and he let me use it. So at least for a time I was saved because I was able to sing instead of preach, and to my surprise I actually announced what I was going to sing all by myself.

In truth, the service went rather well, and afterward I was treated to a nice meal of something. I don't know what it was, but it was something, and it didn't taste all that bad. After lunch I was told a member of the church would drive me back because Pastor Ben had to perform a wedding within the hour, and there wasn't enough time for him to take care of the nuptials and take care of me.

So I said farewell to my newfound friends, some of whom I still write today, and jumped into the member's dilapidated old jeep, only to discover that the thing would not start. Apparently my prayer for engine failure arrived late to the Lord's desk, but being a good God, He always answers our prayers, so we couldn't start that thing with all of us laying our hands and a foot or two on it. So believe it or not, I was handed a few pesos and a map.

What followed is one of the neatest and scariest ninety minutes of my life.

After my sight and hearing returned, the first thing I did was squeeze myself into a bicycle's sidecar. Once I wedged myself in, I was taken to what appeared to be a main street to find a jeepney, if I could. By the way, a jeepney is a real long jeep with twenty to thirty ornery and often smelly people packed in the back.

As it turned out, I couldn't find one. It was Sunday, after all, so I got into the side car of a motorcycle. They call them trics. We drove for about twenty minutes or so, and trust me, there are very few things in the Philippines that a six-foot-tall man can fit into, and the sidecar of a motorcycle isn't one of them. After a while the driver stopped. I paid him, found a little mustard oil, and pried myself out of the thing. And then, thank God, I found myself a pagan jeepney driver willing to drive on Sunday. So I jumped in.

The jeepney, my new conveyance, was all decked out with graffiti, most of which dealt with astrology and the rest of which I dare not repeat. Once inside, I rode in the thing for thirty minutes or thereabouts, and when it finally stopped the driver told me the train station was about eight blocks that way. I paid him and took a walk on the wild side to the train station, admittedly scared to death the whole way. To my surprise I made it to the train station, no worse for wear. I bought a ticket from the pretty lady and waited for the train.

I discovered that train stations and airport terminals are the same everywhere. They are cheaper than a movie and much more entertaining. You ought to just go, sit, and watch sometime.

I was a little disappointed when the train arrived, but I got on board anyway with about ten thousand people, none of whom were in a good humor and some of whom hadn't bathed for a while.

We flew like a bat out of torment for about fifteen minutes while I looked for my stop number, which can be hard to see at Mach 3. Thank God, my stop did finally show up, and I fell out of the train along with a flood of other folks.

So I had traveled all the way across Manila, all by myself, in everything that has ever rolled, it seemed. I had at last arrived less than a mile from my destination, and I was totally lost. I didn't have a clue. The map didn't have the place on it, and besides, we had arrived the night before after dark.

I asked several people, but nobody knew the place I was asking about. Now I was truly upset and starting to pout. I could just see myself lost forever in the bowels of Manila.

When all at once, I heard someone call my name. I looked all over and finally spotted a fella whom I have grown to love like a brother over the years. He was trying to get my attention. His name is Percy, and he was my savior that day and soon to be a lifelong friend.

God is indeed a jokester, but He is good. Amen!

"The Lord will guide you always; he will satisfy your needs in a sun-scorched land and will strengthen your frame. You will be like a well-watered garden, like a spring whose waters never fail" (Isaiah 58:11 NIV).

The Life of Faith

Have you ever had one of those days when for the life of you, you just could not get things to come together? You know, times when no matter how hard you tried, things seemed amiss and confused? Haven't you had a time or two in your life when you looked around and tried to find a place to rest, or to hide, and there was no place to be had?

As I sit at this keyboard, I am having one of those times. I know I am supposed to be witty or engaging. Much to my amusement, I am supposed to lay some pastoral wisdom at your doorstep with this writing, knowing full well that the name Tony Rowell is anything but synonymous with wisdom. When I sit at this desk, something of substance is supposed to come flowing from my mind and onto the paper, and yet I've got nothing, nada, just a blank page and a mind that refuses to slip into gear.

I figured if I just started writing, something would come—you know, like a modern-day Abraham of literature: "Get up and start writing, Tony, and when you are halfway through, I will tell you what it is all about." Well, apparently I am not halfway through. That being said, I know I must carry on. It's my job, after all. I can't just sit here and mope. But what am I to do? My mind is refusing to work with me. My gray cells have all gone black. Instead of a lightning storm in my head as the synapses fire willy-nilly, I have a beautiful clear evening going on. As my Granny would say, I am in a pickle.

I actually just considered going off on a tangent about how to make pickles. Trust me, it isn't easy. I've tried.

I suppose I will have to keep on writing. I will either write until you lose patience and give up on me or something coalesces in my mind. I have to admit, though, that I am a bit frustrated. I was under the impression that if I was willing to do His will then God would give me a better idea of what that will was. Man, that didn't come out right. Let me rephrase that. I believe if I am willing to attempt to understand and follow God's will in a matter, then He will help guide me in my pursuit. That sounds better.

Have you ever felt like that? Frustrated with God, I mean. Don't you have times when you wonder, like me, what God is up to? I sure hope so. I would hate to think I was rowing this boat all by myself.

Being a Christian is hard enough without having to wonder what we are supposed to do next, isn't it? Now don't get me wrong. I remember the Golden Rule and that Christ wants all of us to love one another. Nonetheless, there are times when I sure would appreciate some more specifics. How about you?

Well, believe it or not, I think a revelation of sorts is beginning to dawn in my mind. Perhaps, just perhaps, God's will is for you and me to develop so much trust in His goodness that we don't worry about the details. Perhaps Christ wants our trust to be so great in Him that the who, what, when, and wherefores pale in comparison to the "will."

Christ wants His people to be in the business of doing His will even when we are not sure of what He is doing or our part in it. Our lives are to be undergirded with a solid, unshakable faith in Christ and His goodness. We are to be attempting His will at every opportunity.

Sometimes we are simply called to start writing and see where it leads. We are always called to live for Christ and His kingdom at every moment, even the confusing ones.

So when you start wondering what Christ is up to, remember He knows, and that should be enough. That is called faith, and a life of faith is a life well spent.

Methodist Church in Cades Cove, by Tony Rowell

The Sabbath

I will never forget one blazing hot Sunday afternoon a long time ago, when I wanted a Coca-Cola and I wanted it bad, but Granny didn't have any. So being the first-rate pain I was, I determined to get her to drive down to the store a mile or so away to get me one.

She said: "No. It's Sunday, and other than church and family, we stay at home and rest. Besides, Coca-Cola just isn't good for you."

But I didn't want to rest, and I didn't care what was good for me. I wanted a Coke, and I wanted it bad. So I cajoled and whined, and finally I threw a first-rate seven-year-old fit, and to my amazement she gave in.

She said: "Here's fifteen cents. Go buy yourself one."

Different times back then, you know. A kid was safe enough on the streets, and fifteen cents was still worth fifteen cents.

So off I went, proud as a peacock. I had won a battle against my Granny. It was a proud day for Tony Rowell; let me tell you the truth.

Let me tell you something else—after thirty minutes or so of walking in the midday Florida summer sun, I not only wanted but I needed that Coke. I could taste it. I could feel that ice-cold wonder working its way down my parched young throat. So with great anticipation and a quickened step, I turned the final corner on my journey… only to discover the store in which my treasure lay was closed on Sundays, along with everything else.

I didn't know any of the words back then, but Granny got an imaginary earful nonetheless.

After what seemed like hours, I finally dragged myself back home, only to find Granny waiting for me. In her right hand she had one of those old metal drinking glasses, sweating from the heat, filled with Southern wine (sweet iced tea), and on her face she held a nasty grin filled with satisfaction. Lesson delivered, never to be forgotten.

"Why don't you go out on the front porch and take a nap, like the Lord tells you to."

I joke about it, but in truth it was wonderful back then. Everybody closed on Sunday, because social convention demanded it. After all, it was the Sabbath.

We rested our bodies and filled our souls, because it was the thing to do. We went to church because Momma told us to and we rested, because there was nothing else to do.

A short 10 years later, when I was seventeen or so, most everything was closed on Sundays, as well, but only because the blue laws of South Carolina demanded it. Bible belt, you know.

Well, ten years after that, we ran those blue laws out of town, because we didn't want the government interfering with our God-given right to disobey our God.

Oh, I can feel the hackles rising as I write this.

Now everything is open on Sunday, because there is nothing special about Sunday anymore. It's just like every other day. We run after sports and entertainment and anything else we want on Sunday just like I ran after that Coca-Cola all those years ago, only the store is open now. It's the lesson that's missing.

The day of the Lord is now our day to do with as we wish.

We won! Good for us?

I doubt it.

We Ought To Be Committed

My Granny and Grandpa Tharpe were avid Atlanta Braves fans, even through the bad years. Make that especially through the bad years. I will never forget as a child sitting in my Granny's old house, nestled safe and sound under one of her hand-crocheted afghans, and watching the Braves lose.

Night after night we would come in from fishing or whatever we had been doing and take up our positions: Granny in her old glider rocker and Grandpa on the end of the couch nearest the propane heater. No, he wasn't cold natured, his ashtray was on top of it, and Grandpa was seldom to be seen without an unfiltered Pall Mall cigarette within reach. I sat on the other end of the couch or the floor, depending upon my mood.

Granny would grab her *National Enquirer* magazine to make sure I didn't pick it up and get corrupted. She never read it; she just kept it in her lap so I couldn't get at it. I had to be satisfied with that era's version of the *Oriental Trader* catalog, or if the stars were lined up just right and Granny was really into the game, I could look at the *National Geographic* magazine. A boy never quite knows what he might come across in *National Geographic*.

We would sit there, and I would listen as Granny talked to the television. Grandpa was for the most part silent, but Granny kept up a running commentary on the ills of the other team, the errors of the Braves, and the eyesight of the umpires.

She knew every player by name, where they lived and where they came from, and she had plenty of advice for them if they were to fall into a slump.

From Hank Aaron to Dusty Rhodes and all the way to Tito Francona, I was convinced—as was my Granny—that if they would just listen to her the team would turn around and make something of themselves.

My grandparents' commitment to their team was truly something to behold. Throughout my childhood and well into my thirties, the scene was re-enacted time and time again, and time and time again as the Braves would lose, Granny would shrug it off and say, "We'll get 'em tomorrow!"

That dedication, that commitment was simply part of their being. For if they devoted themselves to something—be it a baseball team on a decades-long losing streak or the Saint Andrews Methodist Church—nothing, and I mean nothing, could shake their resolve. If they committed to something, they stuck to it. They never gave up, and they never gave in.

Every Sunday morning, rain or shine, hot or cold, in the mood or out, Granny put on her best frock, forced me to wash behind my ears, checked my fingernails for dirt, and dragged me to church whether I liked it or not, or for that matter whether she liked it or not.

"You can't always do what you want to do," she said, "Sometimes you just have to do what is best!" To Granny, learning of and worshiping God Almighty was the best, and nothing would stand in her way.

You know, I think sometimes Jesus Christ, our Creator, would be happy if in this era you and I simply treated Him and worshiped Him with half the fervor and commitment we show to our sports teams, our sitcoms, our political parties, and ourselves.

I have considered in the past selling season tickets to worship services in the faint hope that they would sell, but I abandoned that idea for fear that the commitment to attend regularly, implied in the sale, would prevent the sale.

I have been accused in the past of being a little too direct sometimes. I disagree. I believe that direct is often best. Beating around bushes bruises the bushes to no good purpose, and wastes our time on top of that. So let me state a few things rather plainly.

First of all, if you are a parent of young children and your children are anywhere other than the house of God each and every Sunday morning, then I daresay your children are being done a great disservice.

If you are a parent of children old enough to make their own decisions in such matters and you are not in the house of God yourself each and every Sunday morning, then your example—and believe me, no matter how old they are, you are still their primary example—is going wanting.

For grandparents and great-grandparents alike, the statement still holds true.

The Lord in His benevolence has given each of us 168 hours per week to enjoy. If we, as the children of God, cannot spend 1.79 percent of that time, and that includes a one-hour commute, paying homage to the One who gives us physical and eternal life; then I daresay our priorities are in desperate need of adjustment.

Commitment to Christ and His church is lacking in many quarters these days, and the results of that lacking can be seen on any newscast or in any newspaper as the moral decay that surrounds us is plain to see.

Our children, yours and mine, are at risk. We turn a blind eye to that truth to our children's peril. As my Granny would say "Sometimes you just have to do what is best!"

With that in mind, I look forward to seeing you and your family at church on Sunday morning—each and every Sunday morning.

Tug of War!

It was a searching look I saw before me. As I gazed across the divide between us, I discovered the eyes of my opponent were reaching into mine, trying to gauge my strength, my resolve, my determination. I returned the favor and got little reading. His eyes were veiled, as were my own. In those glassy black eyes of his, I saw my own reflection and little else. And I knew that this was not to be simply a battle of physical strength but that my spirit, my will, my strength of character were to be tested—and for a moment, I faltered. My heart quailed at the task before me. Then the humiliation of the sack race flashed in my mind, and I felt within me the rising of a power like none before and none since. I knew then that Pastor Juan and his ragged band of Colombians were going down.

My grip tightened with a Herculean strength. I heard my voice, strong and sure, barking out the order to prepare for battle. I felt the roughness of the manila rope in my palm as the sharp fibers found traction against my skin. I leaned back slightly and felt the team mirror my action. The tension grew as the rope began to tremble beneath our hands.

And then to my left came the cry "Comenzar!"—begin—and the battle was on.

The shock of the initial surge from the Colombians staggered us, but we quickly recovered from the surprise, and just as quickly were staggered again. We were out-matched. The bulging biceps and grim expressions of our opponents left little doubt in our minds what the final result of this little foray into the Colombian camp would be.

But then in a flash of inspiration one of my lieutenants, in a voice strong and clear, began to count, and on the count of three we surged as one. As the cadence continued unabated, the expressions of smug confidence on those before us began to crumble, for the realization was dawning that a bunch of skinny, out-of-shape gringos were besting this group of burley mountain men.

Surge followed surge. Heave followed heave, and finally, as the Colombian sun shone down upon us, first Pastor Juan, then Hugo, and then the rest tumbled across the line defeated and more than a little surprised.

All ended well, though, for the tug-of-war defeat balanced the shame of the sack race, and the scales of justice were as they should be once more. With balance restored, we all left that Sunday afternoon arm-in-arm, brothers and sisters in Christ.

It is amazing what teamwork can accomplish. Things thought impossible are made possible by the concerted effort of a group of people with focus and determination.

In a world where men and women of true Christian strength and character are so greatly needed and so seldom found, my prayer is that we will all simply do what is expected of us. For when one falters, the whole group suffers. Remember that every hand is needed on the rope, for while we may be weak and vulnerable as individuals, we are strong and invincible as a body of believers.

So let's all grab on, lean back, and take care of business for Christ.

Integrity

I have often talked and written of my Granny and Grandpa Tharpe, my mom's folks, as I have tried to relate what truths I could from the Word of God. I have mentioned Mom and Dad, as well, and some of the lessons they taught me that helped produce the man I am today, for good or bad. I have even mentioned my Grandmother Rowell from time to time when it suited the lesson.

But there is one member of the family I seldom, if ever, have mentioned and that would be my Grandpa Rowell—Willie Waldo Rowell, by name.

This failure on my part is not because of any bad memories or anything of that ilk. It simply stems from the fact that I was not able to get to know my Grandpa Rowell very well before he suffered a stroke back in 1972, when I was still little more than a boy.

During my childhood, Grandma and Grandpa Rowell had an interesting relationship. To tell the truth, I never quite figured it out. All I remember is Grandma was always to be found out at the beach cottage a few miles down the road from the Hathaway Bridge in Panama City Beach, while Grandpa frequented a single-wide trailer on the outskirts of Tallahassee. He said he had to stay there for work, even though I was never sure what business Grandpa was in. I do know at one time in his life he owned the Nash and Rambler dealership in Panama City, and that he worked in the government doing something or other. He never struck me as the secret agent type, but who knows?

I have always held to the belief that the trailer was a refuge of sorts for Grandpa. You see, according to my mom, Grandpa was a bit of a rascal, and Grandma was the definition of a Florida blueblood, if ever there was one. How they ever got together only the Lord knows, but I'm glad they did, or I would only be half the man I am today.

To tell the truth, I only really knew Grandpa Rowell after the stroke, and as sometimes happens, the stroke left Grandpa confined to a wheelchair and none too happy about it. Mom always said Grandpa Rowell was as close as she had ever come to a best friend, so I figure in his prime he must have been something to behold, because my mother had particular taste in people, and she would have set some high standards for friendship.

All that being said, I began to develop my picture of Grandpa Rowell at his funeral. You can tell a lot by a person's funeral. Yogi Berra was once quoted as saying: "Always go to other people's funerals, otherwise they won't come to yours." Unusual logic aside, my Grandpa Rowell must have gone to a lot of other folk's funerals, because they sure turned out for his.

I don't remember anything that was said during the service, but I do remember a line of cars that must have stretched out for miles as folks followed Grandpa to his final resting place. I remember being truly touched by the thought that all those folks would come out to pay their respects to the memory of my grandpa.

Some years passed before I approached my dad and asked him a question I had carried ever since the funeral. On one of those rare occasions when a teenage boy and his father were not at odds, I simply asked why so many people had loved and respected Grandpa. Dad did not hesitate. His answer was succinct and to the point. He simply said, "My father was a man of his word."

That didn't mean much to me back then, to be honest. But as I have grown into adulthood and made my way, I have come to understand just how rare a commodity a "man of his word" is in this world. I am proud that my Grandfather Rowell and my father stand in the ranks with such men. I can only hope I can stand so tall.

I suppose the message in all my rambling is simply this: Be who you say you are. Be a man or woman of your word. If you claim it, be it. If you claim Christ as your Lord and Savior, then live like it. "Simply let your 'Yes be Yes,' and your 'No, No.' Anything beyond this comes from the evil one" (Matthew 5:37).

In a world where dishonesty and lack of commitment are watchwords, being a man or woman of your word is one of the best witnesses you can be for Christ. I know it sounds simple, and it is, but never compromise your integrity. Always live as Christ would have you live, and perhaps one day your grandson or granddaughter will marvel at the line of cars following you home.

Broken Pieces

Years ago, my brother, sister, and I headed down to Panama City, Florida, to meet with my father and several other members of the family to say a few words over my Momma and finally lay some of her remains with the remains of her parents, Granny and Grandpa Tharpe.

I don't know how many of you know it, but my mother was cremated. To begin with, I didn't care for the idea too much, but after a bit of reflection, I have come to appreciate the gift Momma gave all of us in her final request. As she lay dying, she requested her remains not be laid to rest in one place, but rather to be divvied up and spread over several different places.

To me, she requested a portion of her ashes be spread over Cades Cove up in the Smoky Mountains. Now, Cades Cove is one of my favorite places. The peace and serenity of the place is beyond compare, not to mention the beauty. Many times over the years, Momma, Dad, and the family would slowly make our way around the cove, counting deer and hoping that, just once, a bear would show itself. My family has continued that tradition.

To my brother, Mom requested a portion of her remains be spread over the waters of Whiskey Slough. Now, Whiskey Slough is a place where Mike and I and my Granny and Grandpa spent many hours fishing in those wonderful years of childhood. Whiskey Slough is just a bit of a turnoff on the Chipola River down near Wewahitchka, Florida. I cannot begin to count the times we all drove down on a Wednesday morning at the crack of dawn to Willis Landing to put in at the river and head for Whiskey Slough. The joyful memory of just sitting there watching my cork and listening to the quiet wind blow through the cypress will forever be a place I go in my mind to escape from the hectic life I lead. I can still recall times when Granny, Grandpa, and I sat for hours, not catching a thing, and not caring.

To my sister, Mom asked that a portion of her remains be placed behind the house near Lexington. You see my sister wasn't one for fishing and the like. She was raised a few years after Mike and me, and by then Granny and Grandpa were slowing down and the fishing was less frequent. Jane spent most of her time at home, so her memories lived in that house and the surrounding land. Jane lives a stone's throw away from Mom's place, and as Mom got weaker, Jane took the lead in caring for her. Many times she would leave her home to go down to Mom and do whatever needed to be done for Momma. Jane's love for Mom was displayed through her actions.

She also asked Jane to put some of her remains out along Thomas Drive on Panama City Beach. Now, Thomas Drive is the main drag down there, and a great deal of my mother was formed along that road. It was where she spent her teenage years. It was where she first fell in love. It was home.

Over the past week, Dad, Jane, Mike, and I made the tour of the Panama City area and fulfilled my mother's request. On Thursday morning, Dad, Mike, and I headed for Wewahitchka and Willis Landing, while Jane headed for the beach. When we reached Wewa, the first thing we did was head for the dam that spans the Dead Lakes. I have written often of my adventures there with my grandparents, of the fishing and fun.

As I walked that dam one more time, I remembered some of the most wonderful times I had as a child. I remembered leaning over that dam hunting for the elusive fresh water mullet. I remembered catching countless fish. I remembered a time when life was one long summer, a time when the simple pleasure of doing nothing was thrilling. I remembered what was truly important in this life: family, friends, and love.

Early on Thursday afternoon, Mike, Dad, and I boarded a borrowed boat and headed down the river to Whiskey Slough. As we pulled into the entrance, I was once again flooded with memories, each and every one of them filled with joy. When we finally drifted to a stop, Mike opened the box and sprinkled a portion of the ashes into the water, followed by Dad. As for me, I held the boat steady and simply watched as the remains of the one from whom I received my life slowly settled to the bottom of a place loved by Mom, and her mom and dad, and her son.

As I watched, a bit of my pain and sorrow settled to the bottom as well. As Mom's ashes intermingled with the muddy waters of home, I once again became her child. Not the child of a mother who is lost, but of a mother who continues to help me deal with the pain of life. In this particular case, the pain of her parting.

At that moment, I realized that in spite of my self-control, in spite of the measure of my mother's strength within me, I am a broken man. Healed a bit by the love and wisdom of a mother who knew how hard saying goodbye would be, but broken nonetheless.

Thank God that He heals the wounded heart!

The Bear Whisperer

It was one of those days just made for hiking. The temperature was hovering around sixty-five or so, the wind was light, and the air enjoyed that particular brand of clarity that only comes from a combination of altitude and last night's rain. As I walked, the sunshine filtered through the poplar and sycamore leaves laying a patchwork of dappled light on the forest floor. The light was playing with my vision a bit, so as I headed down the narrow trail, my attention was focused more upon my feet than my surroundings. I was unfamiliar with the trail, you see, and didn't want to fall down the mountainside upon which I traveled.

It was an odd trail, not well kept and not well thought-out. It was just a simple shelf carved into the mountainside. Trails in the Smoky Mountains are usually well kept and tend to follow natural features that favor the hiker, making the trek longer sometimes, but saving sinew and muscle for another day. This trail, on the other hand, favored no one. It was a very narrow footpath designed for utility, a straight line between point A and point B—nothing fancy.

Between the uneasy lighting and the doubtful footing, my mind was engrossed in placing one foot in front of the other as I traveled. So absorbed was I that I failed to notice a vaguely familiar scent on the wind. When at last instinct jolted me from my single-minded pursuit, the musty smell was much too close for comfort, as was the creature who produced it.

I stopped dead in my tracks to try to locate the offending party when, from around the next bend, a full-grown black bear ambled into sight. He was about fifteen to twenty feet directly in front of me enjoying a leisurely stroll, as was I.

It would seem his attention was elsewhere, as well, for he appeared to not notice me at first. Then, thank God, my offensive odor woke him from his reveries, and he stopped dead in his tracks ten feet or so away, looked up, and regarded me curiously.

To this day I remain fascinated at just how much the human mind can absorb in a millisecond. All I need to do is close my eyes, and I see that grizzled face plain as day.

The first thing I noticed was his eyes. They were not threatening; interested, to be sure, but there was no malice in them. In truth, concern was the overarching impression I received. He wanted to continue, and this gangly human was in the way. He didn't know me from Adam, and a lack of familiarity breeds suspicion in all creatures, so he was watching me with an alert if not vaguely tired expression in his eyes.

The next thing I noticed was the gray around his muzzle. He was a seasoned bear. He was simply taking his morning stroll. Loosening up the kinks, I suppose. That gray had migrated to the fur around his eyes, as well. Perhaps that was the frame that brought out the weary expression I had noticed.

Then there was the rumpled appearance of the skin around his neck. Age had placed a little extra baggage on his frame. I guess none of us are immune from the ravages of time, not even bears.

Finally, I noticed his right ear was in tatters. A badge of honor from days gone by, I suppose.

So there we were. Face to face, nose to muzzle. I don't know about the bear, but my level of concern at that moment was fairly high. I was in a bit of a predicament. I had no desire to remain on that skinny little shelf with that bear, but what was I supposed to do?

I could try backing up, but I was just as likely to step right as wrong and end up lying in the middle of the trail, and I had no desire to set the breakfast table for my friend. I could simply just turn right and jump. The mountain side was only at a thirty-degree angle or so, so the worst that could happen would be a few broken bones. That didn't appeal to me, either.

So I asked myself, "What would an idiot do?" After consulting with myself, an authority on the subject, I decided a twofold approach was best. I would place one foot on the side of the mountain ready to catapult myself down and away, and with the other foot I decided to break all the rules and see what might happen if, instead of backing up, I proceeded forward. The results continue to astound me.

I had no sooner leaned in to move my foot forward when my friend's expression of mild interest coupled with concern changed to concern coupled with terror, and with a pitiful cry he catapulted himself down the side of the mountain. As he rolled, the crisp sounds of saplings snapping, accompanied by the guttural growls and grunts of the bear as he struck more substantial objects, filled the forest. Finally, he came to rest at the bottom of the mountain, jumped to his feet, looked up at me apologetically, and then took off like a scalded dog.

In that my legs would no longer support me, I sat down on the trail and considered the happenings of the past few moments.

First of all, I had to laugh a little when I envisioned that old bear trying to explain to his buddies just how an entrée had chased him down the mountain. I have no idea just how big I was in his story, but I am pretty sure that I was not the 165-pound fella who stood in his way that morning.

Then I considered my mortality for a while, decided I didn't want any more of that morning's pie, and worked my way back down the mountain to home and relative safety.

We all face times in our lives when we feel trapped and frightened. There are times when we can't back up, when we can't move forward, and when standing still is not an option. It is at times like these when faith and trust are essential to the life of a Christian.

I am one who contends that moving forward for the Lord and His Kingdom is the only option, even if moving forward produces risk and danger. Christ never said following Him and growing His kingdom would be easy. In truth, He said it would be difficult. He said it would be dangerous; there would be dark alleys and blind curves. That being said, he also promised to never leave us orphaned. He promised to always see us through.

We will all face challenges as we move forward for the Lord. As we follow the Holy Spirit into the unknown, we may become frightened and want to turn back to the safety of the past; but we must remain true to the cause. We must overcome our fears and venture into the future and the promises that await us there.

What Would Granny Say?

My Granny Tharpe was not what one might consider proper in the way society defines proper. She was a bit gruff and a bit tough and altogether one of the neatest people I have ever known. She was such an odd combination of tenderness and toughness, of kindness and strictness, of femininity and "don't mess with me," that figuring out what she was going to do next was not the easiest thing to do. But in certain instances, there was no doubt.

When I was a kid and we were down at the Dead Lakes helplessly watching as three young men drowned in a whirlpool; or when my brother's appendix ruptured and came very close to killing him; or when the day was particularly pretty; or when the mood just hit her ... at such times, she would rush into action and pray.

I don't recall her being particularly religious, strictly speaking. Yeah, she would go to the Saint Andrews Methodist Church every Sunday, with the express purpose of sitting behind my Grandmother Rowell and pestering her, but aside from that she wasn't one to attend circle meetings or serve on committees. She was what I call a blue-collar Christian, living the simple life of loving her family and her God. When the need arose, however, she would pray, and she didn't care who was around or what anyone, and I mean anyone, thought about it. Granny was, for lack of a better term, unwavering in all she did.

Now the Bible was not often read aloud at Granny's house, but to the best of my recollection, it was never dusty, either. In the privacy of her time with God, Granny read His Word and knew what He expected, and through the eyes of a loving grandson, she didn't appear to disappoint Him all that often. As I have watched the world go from bad to worse since Granny's passing, I have wondered what my Granny would have thought about the current state of affairs.

I can't say she ever had much use for the government to begin with, but when our government started attacking God in schools, on the city square, and over the airwaves, Granny got angry. Granny lived with my mom and dad for a year or so before her passing, and during that time, she and I talked about such things. She was, to say the least, appalled. Now with the escalation of the attacks on the Christian faith, I wonder what she would say to you and me. What advice would she give to help fit us for battle?

As I thought about it, it came to me what her first response would be. Her first response, I have little doubt, would be a simple question directed at those of us who claim Christ as our Lord and Savior. She would look each and every one of us in the eye and without a hint of self-consciousness she would ask:

"So tell me, what are you doing at home? Are you reading the Bible or the TV Guide? Are you praying at any time other than the few well-rehearsed words you say over your meals? Do you offer anything other than lip service to God? Where is God in your life? How can you expect your children to pray in school or at a ball game, or anywhere else for that matter, when you have not taught them how to pray in their own home? Never forget that change starts at home. Fighting for prayer in school, a nativity scene on the courthouse lawn, and the like is all well and good, but praying at home has always been available and seldom is it exercised."

God's Word is available, I daresay, in every household where this writing has found rest, and yet I'll bet you the majority of the Bibles are left dusty and forgotten. Just ask yourself, "When was the last time I opened God's Word at home?" Ask yourself, "When was the last time I opened the Word of God?"

Fight for prayer at school and at ball games and anywhere else where the freedom of religion is threatened, but remember this: Before you can go into the world and fight for God, you must first fight for Him in your own home.

I believe that is what Granny would say, or near-abouts, at least.

I can hear her voice and see her weatherworn face right now in my mind's eye. I can see those black eyes staring into mine. I can sense the years and the wisdom in her stare, and I can feel the shame welling up in me as I thank God that she is not present to hear my answer. How about you?

Whiskey Slough

Whiskey Slough is a magical place for me. It's filled with mystery and mosquitoes, memories and moccasins, alligators, allegories, and the cool green shade of summers past. When life begins to weigh upon my soul, I often find myself journeying back some fifty years or so to a memory nestled beneath the outstretched arms of the cypress. As is evident by the previous sentence, I find myself waxing poetic about the place from time to time, as well.

In my mind's eye, the dappled morning light reflecting off its coffee-colored water puts me in mind of the deep bronze of my Granny Tharpe's face. By midsummer, Granny's Creek roots were in their full glory, and that deep reddish-brown Native face of hers, counterbalanced by an ever-present smile, will forever live in my memories. Granny loved Whiskey Slough.

For those unfamiliar, a slough is a bit of a river that has decided to take a break from the daily grind. Being less flighty than the rest of the water, it finds itself a little depression to the right or left of the river and, making a detour, calls that depression home. The quieter water and ever-present shade are an irresistible calling card for every critter imaginable, including small boys and old ladies with a bit of swamp in their souls and mud in their veins.

It was mid-July as I recall, and for some reason Granny and I had the old rented jon boat to ourselves. Where Grandpa was, I can't recall. Perhaps, being one month into my summer's stay, Grandpa needed a break. Just why that would be the case, I have no idea, but his whereabouts on that midsummer's day remain a mystery.

The sun was blazing down upon us as we paddled down the river that morning. Though it was early in the day, it was easy to trace the sweat as it traveled from armpit to waist, only to pause there for a moment's reflection before continuing on its way. I could go on, but you get the idea. It was hot enough to give the devil pause.

As we paddled on, a familiar crook in the river appeared through the morning mist, and we quickened our pace a bit, for Whiskey Slough and its deep green promise lay just around the bend. I backpaddled to turn us while Granny sculled to guide us, and pretty as you please, we slipped into a little boy's dream.

As the boat slowly drifted to a stop, a medium-sized gator watched us from the bank with little interest. It would appear we caused him no concern, or he was just too hot to move. Either way suited us, if it suited him, or perhaps he recognized Granny from a previous encounter and remembered that just below the gunnel Granny kept a stout, short-handled paddle with which she would dissuade any gator who appeared to have unprincipled thoughts. One way or the other, there was an uneasy détente at play between Granny and the gators, for it would be a sturdy gator indeed who would risk being on the business end of that paddle when Granny's aim was right.

We had a couple of favorite fishing spots in the slough, and Granny headed left so I could tie the bow up to an old familiar friend. To the left of the gator was a particularly tall cypress knee about eight or so feet off the shore, with a groove worn into it from decades of fisherman's knots. Granny pushed the little boat up against it, and from years of practice, I deftly tied us up while Granny dropped the old Maxwell House can filled with concrete over the side, and we set to fishing.

Whiskey Slough appears for all the world like it could have been the primeval birthplace of the piscine Adam and Eve. It's perfect. It's cool and inviting. The water is that ideal shade of blackish brown that portends a great day of fishing. The breeze is gentle and carries with it the faint aroma of wisteria, and the fish are plentiful, and experts at mocking fishermen.

Every fisherman knows that, given the right set of circumstances, a fish can make you look like a fool. You know they are there. They know you are there. They know their place in the food chain as do you, but there are days when they just won't cooperate. They'll show themselves. They'll seductively sidle up to your bait; and just when you think that bobber is going down, they look up, give you a sardonic smile, and it's off to the races.

That's the kind of day Granny and I were having. After an hour and a half of being toyed with, Granny and I were both disgusted and ready to try something new. Even the gator looked bored.

So while Granny was pulling up the anchor, I worked my way to the front of the boat to untie us. Being partially freed, the current caught the boat and swung it in the direction of the gator, who began to show renewed interest in the two of us and me in particular, since I was the smallest of the fare.

This served as a bit of a distraction, so I failed to notice that while there had been only a single manila rope tying us to the knee initially, now there were two—and a lively rope it was. As I reached out to loosen us up, a streak of light-brown greased lightning flew past my cheek, ruffled my hair a bit, and then disappeared into the depths beyond with barely a ripple to indicate his visit.

To this day, I don't know if Granny witnessed this. I believe she did, though. As I recall, her bronze face took on a slight brassy hue, and she was quieter than usual for a while. That being said, she asked me what I was waiting for and calmly watched me untie us, all the while keeping an eye on the gator and a hand on that paddle of hers.

Meanwhile, I was thanking God that somewhere beneath that old jon boat swam a cottonmouth with astigmatism.

I know I was supposed to tell this story, but as I wrote it I kept wondering why. I understand memories are more valuable to those who hold them than they are to others, but I felt compelled to put pen to paper and write this down.

Perhaps it's simply a reminder to pay attention, for like that gator, given a chance Satan can be awakened and spurred to action. Simply put, be sure to keep yourself from drifting in his direction, for like the snake when he decides to act, he is swift. But unlike the snake, he often hits his mark. So be careful out there.

Granny Tharpe and Grandma Rowell

Latvian Morning, Tasi, Latvia, by Tony Rowell

Diamonds and Stones

At last I had found peace—peace and quiet and a calmness of spirit I hadn't felt for a long time. It was late summer back in 2006, and my ordeal of prostate cancer was almost over. At least, the surgery and acclimating myself to the changes in my life were nearly over. That being said, I was still struggling a bit mentally over the physical alterations brought on by the situation, but spiritually speaking, I had reconciled myself to the current state of affairs and God's hand in all of it. The hand of God was evident in the calming of my fears and in the help received as I struggled with my all-too-evident mortality.

I was traipsing through one of my favorite locales, one that I had last visited the day before heading down to Charleston for the aforementioned surgery. On that day, five or so months earlier, I had gone over to one of my childhood haunts, the old Porth pond, to do a bit of illegal-ish fishing, to do a little reminiscing about the joys of childhood, and to try to forget about the coming day.

The illicit fishing went well, as I recall, with a couple of nice largemouth and a catfish or two making their reluctant way to the shore. Being little more than a child myself, the reminiscing was pretty successful, as well, but the forgetting part left me wanting.

On this day however, five months later, I was doing fine. The dreadful fear was a thing of the past. The surgery and its side effects were fading, and life was good. My heart was light, my spirit was rising, my body was on the mend, and my stringer was filling up with shellcracker and bream. The nightmare was coming to a close.

There are times in this life when the Lord grants His children a glimpse of the peace and joy that awaits them over the Jordan, and this was one of those moments for me. I have always pictured heaven as a well-stocked farm pond.

Relishing the closing of the day, I listened as the night sounds began. I heard a faint croak over to my left, deep in the reeds, and that was all that was needed for innumerable frogs to start calling to one another in the dusk. How they sort out who is who, I will never know. The crickets and other creepy crawlies of the swamp were in romantic moods themselves, and together they joined one another in their shadowy mating calls. In some, this weird symphony might produce misgivings, but in me it produced calm.

As the sun sank and the shadows lengthened, I daydreamed of summer evenings past. Other such evenings when similar sights and sounds had held me close and comforted me. And as I dreamed, I cast my bait about nonchalantly in the hope that perhaps there was one more nibble to be had before the darkness drove me homeward.

All was shadows and silhouettes when, to the right and a little behind an old stump, the water swelled, wrinkling the surface and sending out the telltale concentric rings which indicate prey. With a stutter step to the left to clear the pathway and an instinctual movement of the wrist, I sent my deep blue six-inch Culprit rubber worm sailing through the night air with pinpoint accuracy toward the center of those rings.

As it took flight, however, an uneasy feeling of impending doom filled my breast—for as I moved a silhouette, previously hidden in the shadows, emerged from the darkness.

The ominous form of a feathery dreidel was hanging from a low-lying branch. In slow motion I watched as my projectile entered one side and exploded out of the other. In an instant that silhouette, so peaceful a moment before, shattered into a thousand pieces, all angry and searching for a place to vent. It took a moment, but as one those hornets, now homeless by my hand, discovered the fishing line. And following it to its origin, they set their affections on me.

Over the years I have faced black bears, razorback hogs, and belligerent parishioners with an aplomb envied by many; but when those enraged hornets balled up and headed my direction, any pretense of confidence, manliness, and macho I may have once possessed vanished in an instant. Throwing my Zebco 33 to the side, I hiked my skirts and headed for the water just as fast as my legs would carry me.

I just about made it, too, but when salvation was at hand, my foot happened to land on a snake. As the startled snake proceeded to dance about under my feet, and I all but levitated trying to get off the thing, my mind quickly assessed the situation and realized that this particular snake was harmless. It was just a big old brown water snake.

While all of this was going on, the hornets had paused to watch the show, but just as soon as the aforementioned snake broke free and slithered into the pond, they renewed their advance.

As they made their final approach and got into attack formation, my mind said, "Jump in. They can't get to you there," while my fear said "Say what? There's a snake in there."

"It's harmless!" shouted my mind.

"Don't care!" countered my fear.

My moment of indecision gave the hornets all the opportunity they needed, and taking full advantage, two or three drove that advantage home into one of the more fleshy parts of my anatomy while another particularly adventurous character managed to get up underneath my fishing vest and go to town. Now that the lesser of two evils had been established, I dove in, hat and all.

Later, cautiously emerging, I found the hornets had headed home to rebuild, the snake had vanished, licking his wounds elsewhere, I suppose, and my hat was nowhere to be found. So, with an embarrassed grin, I sighed and headed home: my peace shattered, my pride tattered, and my rear-end stinging like the devil himself.

Life can be like that sometimes. To quote John Denver, "Some days are diamonds, and some days are stones." I contend that most days are both.

I suppose the key is to make all the diamonds and all the stones count, no matter what. They are all gifts from God above, and gifts are meant to be enjoyed. So cherish the peace and laugh at the turmoil. Enjoy the life God has given you, no matter what. You only get one chance, one life on this earth. Enjoy it, make the most of it, and make every day count. Produce no regrets, only cherished memories.

That's just a little free advice to be taken in a time of need.

What and Why

For more than thirty years now, I have been hauling my carcass all over the world doing mission work of one kind or another. I just love it. I have been on medical missions, construction missions, rescue missions, disaster response missions, and disaster recovery missions and have been greatly blessed each and every time I have gone out. For me it's just as natural as breathing, and I can think of no better way to spend my life than wandering the planet from time to time doing the Lord's bidding; but I also understand that for many the allure of mission work is more of a mystery than it is a miracle.

Someone asked me the other day, "What do you do when you are over there?" That I can answer without so much as a moment's hesitation. We work. We play. We worship. We live our lives with folks different and yet the same as we. We play in an expanded sand box with fellow children of God. To the best of our ability, we fix it if it's broken, soothe it if it hurts, bandage it if it's bleeding, and pray over everything.

Over the past couple of years, my team has been working in the Baltic country of Latvia. Specifically, in Latvia, we are working to help restore the church, which was devastated when the "Iron Curtain" fell upon it, crushing the institution, confiscating its wealth and property, and outlawing its practice.

Through building repair and restoration, we help to rebuild the tradition of the Latvian Methodist church. As the old buildings are brought back to life, traditions—dormant for seventy-five years—have space to grow and blossom once again. Practices outlawed and oppressed for decades are given expression. Institutional memories are revived as structures revered for generations are restored and repopulated with the memories of past matriarchs and patriarchs of the Latvian church.

Through the simple acts of pouring a concrete slab, refinishing an ancient pine floor, and refurbishing a long-neglected fellowship hall, the spiritual lifeblood of the church is replenished. The fire is fed a bit more kindling, and the Kingdom of God here on earth and in heaven is strengthened a bit.

Will the actions of a few good-hearted South Carolinians in Latvia be of any lasting value? I honestly have no idea. I do know whatever we build in a physical sense does indeed have a life span, and in time the floor will need refinishing, the room will need refurbishing, and the concrete will become stained and cracked with age. Such is the way of things.

I also know Christian love has no half-life, for Christian love flows from Christ, and Christ will never tire. Christ and His love are eternal, so the love shared between our Latvian brothers and sisters and ourselves will remain in place to support, nourish, and enliven us all forever.

As to why some are drawn by God to exotic places while others are drawn across the street to do the Lord's work, I have no satisfactory answer for those who question such things. I know it sounds a bit pedestrian, but the Lord has His way. And I know without a doubt that while I cannot fully understand, He does, and that is good enough for me.

Whittling

My Granny and Grandpa Tharpe were two of the best grandparents a kid could ask for, in my opinion. Grandpa was kind and gentle, soft-spoken and graceful in his own way, and since he worked for Borden Dairy, he also had access to Fudgesicles from his truck, which went a long way toward building his status as a first-rate grandpa. Granny was kind and gentle in her own special, forceful way. She was graceful, as well. Soft-spoken would be a bit of a stretch, but I am willing to make it. She baited her own hook, rowed her own boat, and cleaned her own fish, all of which worked in her favor from a little boy's standpoint.

They had a great yard with an old claw-footed, cast-iron bath tub full of dirt and wigglers; catawba trees, complete with catawba worms for fishing; a fence that was not so high you couldn't jump it; and a flower bed full of caladiums and toads. The crème de la crème, however, was a couple of great climbing trees, or shade trees depending on your mood at the time, and that brings me to my subject: Whittling.

It was a sweltering summer's day back in the sixties. It was hot enough that shade trumped climbing, so my older brother, Mike, and I were sitting in the front yard under one of the chinaberry trees. We were sitting in our respective Adirondack chairs watching the odd car go by and chewing the fat like a couple of old men. We each had a glass of iced tea to wet the whistle, a stick, and a knife. We were whittling.

It was on that day I discovered that I would never attain one of my dreams. I was not going to develop into a great sculptor. I was not going to develop into a mediocre sculptor. I was not a going to be a sculptor. Michelangelo, I'm not.

Mike and I were raised in a less cautious, a less paranoid era, and because of that we were sitting in the shade doing our best to turn those sticks into knives. We had war games planned you see, with bulwarks of dirt from the road, grenades from the magnolia trees, dirt clod bombs and, of course, our shimmering sabers.

We both started with the same material. We both had wood, sharp knives, and time. As time progressed, the shavings piled up around both chairs, the tea slowly disappeared, and under Mike's hands his stick turned into a credible impersonation of a military Ka-Bar knife. In that Mike is detail oriented to a fault, the thing had blood grooves, those little notches on the top, and a pretty sharp edge. He even cut a diamond pattern in the grip so it would be easy to grasp and, of course, he carved his name in it right where the manufacturer would put theirs. It was impressive.

After I took a look at Mike's work of art and made a close examination of it, I turned my attention to what I had produced with the same time, the same wood, and the same carving knife. Upon close examination of my work, I had to admit that I had produced a credible impersonation of a disfigured stick.

So what is the point of this story? Well, it's simple really. We all start off as rough pieces of material, brought into the world through no choice of our own. We don't choose the family, we don't choose the time, and we are essentially helpless.

How we are raised to adulthood is not left up to us, but to others; and sometimes it is done well and sometimes it isn't. We have little control over that. Nonetheless, in all of our lives, we do have choices.

There comes a time when we place ourselves into the hands that will shape us. There comes a time in life when we realize who we are is greatly determined by our allegiances. Not earthly allegiances so much as spiritual ones. Who we choose to ally ourselves with determines not only our final destination, but the final outcome of ourselves.

If we choose to place our lives, ourselves, into the hands of anything other than Jesus Christ, what will be produced is a disfigured impersonation of what was created to be perfection itself. With the shavings of love, peace, joy, forgiveness, and humility scattered on the ground, all that will be left is a hard-bitten shell of what was meant to be.

That being said, remember that the Almighty Sculptor, Jesus Christ, yearns for you to place yourself in His hands. Under His knife, the person you were created to be will emerge. The shavings of pride, greed, and self-seeking will fall away, and a child of God will be born.

It won't be easy. Growth never is. Always remember, however, that you will be in the hands of the God of love—a God who earnestly loves you and passionately desires that you become the shining example of His creation you were born to be.

The only question remaining is, "Whose hands will shape you?"

Trusting

There are few words in the English language that change a person quite like the word cancer. For those of us who have heard that word spoken in relation to ourselves and our condition, the moment it was uttered is branded in our memories.

Mortality rushes in like a flood with fear riding the crest of the wave. For a split second every muscle in your body tightens, and the resulting nausea feels like you just stepped off a rollercoaster after having a seven-course meal. This is quickly followed by disbelief at what you are hearing. Once that subsides, an odd feeling of, "Well, now that's interesting!" creeps in, along with a sense of helpless inevitability.

At least, that is what my heart, mind and spirit experienced when I sat down in my doctor's office several years ago to hear the words, "Now look what you have done, Tony. You have gone and gotten yourself cancer!"

I remained suspended for a time after the doctor's visit within a confused cloud of self-pity, anger, fear, and disbelief. I wondered what I had done to deserve this. What great sin had I committed that brought on this calamity? I was a mess for a time, but all good things must come to an end, and eventually I was able to think rationally again and consider my plight through reasoned eyes.

My reason told me it was simply the luck of the draw. After all, the body is a mechanism, beautifully made, but destined to die in the long run. This cancer of mine was simply the first shot over the bow of my life. It got my attention.

I remember finally getting to the point where praying seemed like a good idea, and every night I prayed for the same thing: an explanation. To this day I have yet to receive one, but explanation or not, I did receive a message, a message that to me was just as direct and clear as if Christ were sitting across the kitchen table from me. The simple message was, "Trust Me."

A simple request to be sure, but honoring such a request when you are preparing to go under the knife, knowing that to awaken means a drastically changed life and lifestyle, is difficult to be sure. I determined to do my best, though.

I will freely admit that after the surgery, the recovery and side effects made trusting Christ more difficult than I could have imagined, but I soldiered on, and trust I did. He pulled me through. Thanks be to God!

I don't intend to belabor the point of trust too much in this writing. Suffice it to say that trusting in Christ is not always easy. Laying your burdens down at His feet, while sounding good in theory, is difficult in practice. But for those of us who call ourselves Christians, such trust is essential.

Difficult times are part of life. You cannot escape them. They will be here just as sure as the sun will rise in the morning, and avoiding them is simply not an option most of the time. So if avoiding difficult circumstances is not feasible, we had best turn to the God of circumstance and trust He knows better than we which way to turn and which way to go.

Life is full of unknowns and uncertainties, and at times all of us can become overwhelmed. At such times, remember the God of circumstances has promised to never leave you orphaned. He will be there every step of the way.

On the other hand, He has never promised to keep you from the challenges of life. It seems that often He allows a hurdle to cross your path with the aim of seeing just how well you will vault over it. For it is in the vaulting that the faith is strengthened and the resolve tempered.

That being said, Oswald Chambers once wrote that God "never has a museum," but rather His life is manifested in the lives of his children. In other words, talk is cheap. It is in the day-to-day challenges that your faith is strengthened and displayed. It is in the ordinary stuff of life where our ability to trust in Christ is best demonstrated to those around us and where the greatest advancements of the Kingdom take place.

The big challenges are made easier if in the small ones we first rely.

So let us all resolve to trust in Christ in all things, the great and small alike. Let us resolve to live out our Christianity in all aspects of life so that Christ's Kingdom is seen by all, and His love and peace are not only spoken of, but also lived and shared.

Words Are Cheap

The best I can recall it was early August, the dog days of summer in the panhandle of Florida, and hot enough to make your eyeballs sweat. I was in Granny's backyard doing what young boys did back then in a time before video games or Ritalin. I was digging holes, looking for catawba worms, whittling this or that, and generally trying to find some mischief to get into.

I was skilled at the task, so it didn't take very long. As I cast about for an evil scheme, I noticed out of the corner of my eye that Miss Irene, Granny's infamous neighbor, had a nice little watermelon patch in her backyard, and there is nothing like a watermelon on a warm afternoon.

I've told y'all about her before. She was a sight. Built like a Frigidaire, about seven feet tall with red eyes. I swear she had red eyes. She always wore a nondescript dirty house frock, and she never washed her hair; she figured cleanliness would alter her mystique, I suppose. She lived in a house that Swamp Witch Hattie would have been proud to call her own, and she had a voice that rattled the windows like a midsummer thunderstorm.

That woman scared your average child silly, but she downright terrified me. I half expected that somewhere in the bowels of her ramshackle house there was a huge boiling pot for rendering children down.

That being said, I was hungry, and those watermelons were calling my name loud and clear just like a mystical siren of old. So I figured, well, you know, maybe I could sneak over there and borrow one of those watermelons when nobody was lookin'.

They looked mighty good. They weren't the big ones; they were those little round ones that sometimes have yellow fruit inside. Now that makes them extra good, but only a skilled watermelon thumper like my Granny can tell if it's yellow or not. So when the coast was clear, I went over there and borrowed one of those watermelons. I fully intended to give it back, I really did. Well, most of it, anyway.

So there I was, sitting under the catawba tree with my back up against the old trunk, enjoying the shade. I was just starting in on that watermelon when Granny wandered out of the house to put the wash on the line, and while hanging up her dainties, she noticed me eating that watermelon.

So she went in and got me a spoon, and one for herself, and we sat down together and thoroughly enjoyed that watermelon. It tasted especially good considering the heat and the company.

We talked about this and that and about how great the watermelon was while we ate, and then she thanked me and said, "Now that sure hit the spot. How much did that set you back?"

I hemmed and hawed for a little while; but in time honesty took over, and I told her that I had, well, pilfered it from Miss Irene's house.

Granny never skipped a beat, and with an evil grin on her face she said, "That's fine, no problem. Just go over and ask Miss Irene what she wants for it, and pay the woman."

Now I was eight years old. I didn't have a dime to my name and didn't have any prospects of getting one. She had me. I told her I was sorry. I told her I would even tell Miss Irene I was sorry if she would go with me, but Granny just grinned and said in that no-nonsense tone I knew so well, "No, no, that won't wash. The proof is always in the pudding. Words are cheap. If you are really sorry then you've got to go apologize, and then pay Miss Irene."

So I spent the entire rest of that day weeding a watermelon patch and cleaning that woman's backyard, worrying for my life the whole time. I swear I could hear a pot of water boiling all afternoon, and I just knew it had my name on it.

I really was sorry by the way, mainly that I got caught, and skillfully at that, but I also knew that I had done Miss Irene wrong and needed to make it right. Granny hadn't dragged me to Sunday school for nothing. On top of that, I also knew that just saying I was sorry wasn't enough. Action was required to balance the books and prove the sorry.

To tell the truth I just wanted to escape into my memories a little today, so I wrote this old story down and let my mind wander back for a time, but there are a couple of lessons that bear pointing out, especially for you parents and maybe even you grandparents out there.

Mainly, don't browbeat your children, but don't let them get away with it, either. Children need direction, and sometimes that might mean they need some hard lessons taught.

I wouldn't recommend acting like a co-conspirator, as my Granny did from time to time, unless of course that's your thing.

But allowing those in your charge to get away with wrong is harmful to them. It will damage them in the long run and make their life much more difficult than it has to be.

I know today the world preaches that wrong is not wrong, that sin is not sin, and nothing is black and white, only gray, but deep down we all know better than that.

So love your children and raise them up in the way they should go. Oh, and just in case you didn't catch the reference, drag those kids to Sunday school on Sunday morning, and stay for awhile yourself.

A good example goes a long way in the mind of a child.

Special Days

Street Dancers (Cartagena, Colombia), by Tony Rowell

Cades Cove, by Tony Rowell

For Mother's Day:
The Coaster

I started out wanting to write to and about all of you moms and grandmas out there in that it's May, and Mother's Day is right around the corner. Now in order to do the subject justice, I felt I needed to get into the role. So I sat down at the keyboard and asked myself, "What is it like to be a mother?"

After spending an hour or so casting about for an answer, I have to admit I have no idea. There are some things you just have to experience for yourself, and in that I am not maternal material, I am at a bit of a loss. But I do remember something Mary said earlier in the evening that could be a good springboard for this article. She said motherhood is like being on a rollercoaster.

I like rollercoasters. When I was a bit younger, I loved to ride them, especially the ones that turn you upside down and inside out. You know, the ones that make you think you just might end up in the next county if you let go. So you let go anyway just to see what happens.

I even like the old wooden coasters that shake, rattle, and roll you till your head spins; Old Thunder Road used to be a thrill to ride until they took it down.

I've been sitting here trying to figure out exactly what Mary meant, and I think I might have a bit of a handle on it. I know this much: Once you strap yourself into a rollercoaster and that bugger starts heading up the hill, you're committed. In truth, that is the only part of a rollercoaster ride that makes me nervous. I suppose it's anticipation mixed with fear that unnerves me, because I know without a doubt that things are about to get crazy.

The slow grind of the chains sounds a bit ominous as you ascend to the top. Then after what seems like hours, the apex is finally achieved; the chains fall away; and for just a moment, an almost imperceptible moment, there is an expectant stillness.

Then with a rush the wind hits you, the sensation of extreme speed grips you, and then comes the uncomfortable realization that you are riding a wave you can't stop. You are out of control. You have become part of the rollercoaster, and you have very little to say as to where it goes. Your only option is to hang on for dear life and do your best to enjoy the ride.

You pray endlessly as the thing tosses and turns you. One minute you're looking at the sky, and the next, the ground rushes at you at an alarming speed. On the outside of the wilder corners, you feel like you just might be flung into space and lost, but thank God, gravity and inertia hold you tight.

Then just as quickly as it started, you feel a lurch as the brakes are applied, and as the car slows down, an odd sense of disappointment and a strange deep-felt sadness that it's over embraces you.

I am not a mom. I'm a dad. But I have watched, and I have to say that being a mother must be one of the most frightening, heart-wrenching, and rewarding jobs in the universe. I know that often you have to feel out of control for yourself and frightened for your children. You don't show it. You hide it, but frightened you are. The task that has been placed upon your shoulders, of raising children in the way they should go, is one of the most daunting and the most important jobs given by God.

I can only imagine the churning within your spirit as you strive to give strength, stability, and love to those under your charge. From time to time I have no doubt you feel as if you might be flung into space and lost.

At times such as these, remember you have a God, a Savior, who strengthens and understands. Rely upon Him and He will strengthen, guide, and protect you. Then when the time comes to relinquish your charges into God's protection, He will hold you close and comfort you in your sorrow; and in time He may bless you with grandchildren.

Then you and they can go play at the waterpark.

Happy Mother's Day.

For Father's Day:
Life in the Brackish Water

It was so hot that you could feel the sweat trickling down your back. If I had been wearing a shirt, it would have been sticking to me, but I was twelve or so, and my wardrobe for the summer consisted of a pair of cutoffs and tennis shoes. As I recall I seldom wore a shirt, but I always wore shoes, ever since the time I stepped on a yellow jacket hole without them and paid the price.

On this particular hot July afternoon, Grandpa Tharpe and I were heading back to the house from Dearpoint Lake. We said we had gone there to fish, but actually we had gone there to get away from my Granny as she prepared for the coming family reunion to be held at her house.

Between the cooking and the coming guests, she was as nervous as the proverbial long-tailed cat in a room full of rocking chairs, and she let it out by being nasty to Grandpa and me from time to time. On account of that, we decided we needed a break, so we took off fishing.

Dearpoint Lake is really interesting. You see, it is situated just a few miles from the coast of the Gulf of Mexico. As a matter of fact, it is separated from Panama City Bay by only a dam. It's one of those dams that has a spillway that is always running, so the water on one side is fresh and on the other, it is brackish. That is, it's a mixture of fresh and salt water.

Now from what I have learned in school and from observation, brackish water is teaming with life. Life that can live nowhere else can live in this strange mixture of waters. If you ever get a chance, go down to the salt marshes on the coast and see what I mean. Unless I am mistaken, Murrell's Inlet, or at least the marshes that surround it, is made up of brackish water for the most part, and those of you who have been there know the life it holds.

Well, at that time in my life, as it is with most budding young men, I was having some difficulties with my dad. Nothing big, mind you, but I was resentful of him being gone all the time. You see, he worked for General Electric at that time and was gone a lot, but I wanted him near, to play ball and fish and to do all the things that boys love to do with their dads.

In truth, I wanted him to be like my grandfather, who always seemed to have time for me. When I was at Grandpa's house, he always seemed available. He always seemed near, seldom scolding, seldom correcting. In truth I resented my father for not being as available and as forgiving as was my Grandpa.

In that Grandpa and I were very close, I told him about my feelings. Make that, he egged me on until I told him what he already knew. So it was that on the way home from fishing on that July afternoon that he decided to try and explain what fatherhood was to me.

Now, my Grandpa wasn't much on words. Actions were his usual teaching method, but this time he told me something that stuck.

First of all, he told me that being a daddy was like always living in the fresh water. You got to play most of the time. Everything tasted good. As a daddy you were always able to make everybody happy. You were always there to play ball, to take walks, to do whatever came to mind. Being a daddy was fun and exciting.

Then he told me that being a father was like living in the ocean. The water was salty and difficult to drink. You were forever trying to fight the surf to get things done. Life as a father was seldom fun. It was usually difficult and tiring. Playing ball was forbidden, walks were scarce, and even though you fought with the current to bring life to your family, the fight was seldom appreciated because they were not out in the water with you. They were waiting on the shore. Life as a father was difficult, to say the least.

Finally, Grandpa told me, life as a dad was like life in the brackish water. He said in the brackish water there was a good mixture of the two—fun and games and hard work and responsibility. He said that life was to be found in the brackish water.

He slowed the truck down a bit and looked me in the eyes when he told me that, when I became a father, I would need to swim for the brackish water as fast as I could. He said the undertow of the ocean was far greater than that of the fresh water, and if I wasn't careful, I would be overtaken by the responsibilities of fatherhood and neglect what was really important. He told me if I wasn't careful, I would sacrifice life for livelihood.

He was quick to point out that both were needed, but that maintaining the mixture, while being hard to do, was the essence of life. He continued to explain to me that my dad was doing his best to raise three children in a world which was constantly changing, and that from time to time the ocean would pull my dad under as it had my grandpa in a similar time of his life. Grandpa explained that he was now free of the burdens of many family responsibilities, and that was why he was able to do what he knew my dad so longed to do with me.

In that few minutes with Grandpa, on that sweltering summer's day back in the 1960s, my life was changed. His words of true wisdom changed my life forever. I continued to wish for more time with Dad, but I at least understood, as much as a twelve-year-old can, the reasons for his absence; and I was therefore able to enjoy his presence all the more.

As time followed its inexorable path, I grew up and became a father. I have struggled to follow my grandfather's advice over the years. I realize I have more often than not spent my time swimming against the current, far from my family.

I write this little note to once again explain to them, my family, the reasons, and to let them know that given a choice, I would rather be with them than with anyone else on the face of the earth.

And to you the reader, especially if you are a dad, take the time to play in the fresh water awhile. Enjoy your loved ones' company to the fullest. Don't waste a minute.

For the minutes are so very few and so very precious.

Grandpa Tharpe and Grandpa Rowell

For Thanksgiving:
The Thanksgiving Conundrum

Since childhood I have pondered the difference between dressing and stuffing. For the past fifty or so Thanksgivings, the subject has crossed my mind. Is it simply a matter of location, or are they actually different? Maybe it's a cultural thing, or perhaps it's a regional thing and semantics are to blame for the confusion. Personally, if I were to be given a vote on the matter, I would go with dressing. It is certainly more appealing to say that this food or that makes the entire meal fancier than it is to imagine ingesting something that emerged from the dark internal recesses of a turkey unprotected by shell. Yep, I'll go with "dressing."

Then there is cranberry sauce. Before I go any further, I will confess a bias against the substance.

When her children were young, my mother found it interesting to have her progeny try different things. In my case, she found a great deal of pleasure in watching me sample various culinary delights. To a casual observer, it would be obvious that the less delightful I found the delight to be, the more delightful my mother found my facial contortions. I have yet to decide if this side of my mother arose from a loving desire to expand my horizons or from the Mrs. Hyde within. Personally, if I were to be given a vote on the matter, Mrs. Hyde would win, but that's just me. One way or the other, Mom's shenanigans stopped when the ambrosia forced upon me at the tender age of seven was returned to sender via airmail. I think the enjoyment was diminished a bit for Mom after that.

One of these experiments dealt with cranberry sauce. I distinctly remember being confused. Was this substance in my mouth a solid or a liquid, animal or vegetable, good or bad, dead or alive? For the life of me I couldn't tell, and that lack of certainty remains with me to this day—and, in turn, I cannot bring myself to revisit the experiment.

Now the Thanksgiving turkey, I understand. Let me explain.

First of all, there are two basic entrées associated with Thanksgiving and Christmas, at least according to my reckoning. As a rule, depending upon the holiday, either a turkey or a ham makes up the bulk of the meal.

Now my mom, being Mom, liked to shake things up from time to time with the likes of raw oysters or burritos, but I think we can all agree Mom had a culinary screw loose. For those of you who prefer adventurous gastronomy, my mom's forays into the epicurean wilderness would have been enchanting, but for those of us who prefer plates with little compartments to separate our dressing from our stuffing and our cranberry sauce from everything else, Mom's wanderings were a certifiable nightmare. But like my mother before me, I find myself wandering. Let me return to the subject at hand: Ham or turkey?

From my observations, I have discovered that, in most cases, ham is reserved for Christmas, while turkey is for Thanksgiving, with the leftovers spanning the month in-between. I have often wondered why these two foods were chosen for such honorable tasks. I think I may have found the reason.

Christmas, Santa Claus aside, is designed to be a celebration of one miraculous and beautiful event: the birth of our Lord and Savior Jesus Christ. Christ, and His incarnation, is why Christmas exists. Without Christ there is no Christmas and, no, I don't care what anyone says about it. Christ is Christmas and Christmas is Christ.

The humble ham is a relatively boring, if not tasty entrée. There is just so much you can do with a ham. From my experience ham tastes pretty much the same no matter from where you take a bite. From the outer edge to the bone the ham is relatively unchanged. It tastes like ham. It looks like ham. It's ham.

Ham is the perfect food when only one thing is being celebrated. There are few distractions when you sit down and eat a ham. There are few decisions to be made when a ham is set before you; thin or thick slices, that's about it. I love ham. It fits well into my entrée compartment.

Now the turkey is another matter altogether. From the dark meat to the white meat, from the breast to the leg, from the neck to the giblets, the turkey has many facets, many tastes, and many textures to revel in and savor. Now in that Thanksgiving is a time to celebrate the myriad gifts that our Lord has rained down upon us, the turkey is the perfect Thanksgiving table centerpiece.

I love Thanksgiving. I love it for several reasons, but for me at least the main reason is family. In my line of work the Christmas season is very busy, and while others enjoy some time off with family and friends, I am often occupied with the various duties that are specific to my chosen vocation during the holiday season. So Thanksgiving is the time when I bask in the glow of family.

Thanksgiving is that one day a year, when I can look around the table and marvel, without distraction, at all the blessings that surround me. Not only that, but I also marvel at the blessed memories that return those long since gone back into the familial fold, as the matriarchs and patriarchs of the past populate the family portrait in my mind.

My prayer for each and every one of you is this: I pray that on this Thanksgiving, no matter your circumstance, no matter your station, you take the time to reflect upon the wonderful gifts God has given you in this life.

I pray we all can take the day, this one day, and be thankful and joyous. We can all return to the pushing and shoving, to the angst and anxiety, and to the incessant clamor of the world later. On this Thanksgiving Day I pray that you enjoy your family, enjoy your friends, and give thanks to the God of peace and love who makes it all possible.

For Christmas:
Celebrate It and Pass It On!

It was sometime around the beginning of October when I began to notice it: the subtle creeping, commercial Christmas. As I recall, Mary and I had headed up to Franklin, North Carolina, to enjoy a couple of days away and to marvel at the fall colors decorating the trees that lined the Blue Ridge Parkway. It was indeed a wonderful time of rest and reflection, a little time to get to know one another again. But as with all good things, this too had to come to an end. In the late afternoon, as we traveled back down the road toward home, the far-off taste of chicken and dumplings began to beckon me.

You see, I knew in the not-too-distant future we would be passing near a Cracker Barrel, and sure enough, in time, the old sign came into view. We pulled into the now familiar parking lot, requested our traditional table with a view, and enjoyed a fine meal together, all the while reminiscing about the joys of the past few days.

After the meal, we wandered around the store a bit looking at the bobbles and bangles they sell. They do have some really interesting things and some pretty original gifts, if you are into that sort of thing. Nonetheless, as we wandered Mary drifted over to the clothes, so I faded back and worked my way over to the toys as is my want in such situations.

It was there that I noticed it. Among the toys was a nondescript little sign reminding me that Christmas was just ninety-some-odd days away, with the implied warning that I had better get this or that toy while it lasted.

At first, I simply assumed that the sign was a stowaway from last year's season, but upon closer examination it appeared to be newly printed and placed. There were no tattered corners, the paper wasn't discolored, and the tape had not yellowed at all. So somebody had actually put that thing up three months before Christmas Day to get the sales going.

It was then I knew I was getting a bit old, for I heard my father speaking when I muttered, "What in the world is the world coming to?" under my breath on the way out to the truck.

Since that time, I have pondered what import the mess we have made of Christmas has had upon Christianity itself. What damage, if any, has been foisted on our faith by a world mad for money and our participation in the madness?

I have often preached that we as believers need to beware of being distracted by the commercialization of Christmas, but upon reflection I don't believe distraction is the greatest problem. I believe that the debasement of Christ and cheapening of the gift of God's grace is a far greater sin.

Just think of it. God has placed the mystery of the incarnation in our hearts through the coming of the "babe in the manger," and we have stood by and allowed the world to put the mystery in a box, wrap it with a bow, and put a price tag on it.

We have even allowed the world to kick Christ off of the public stage, even during the Christmas season. If I hear one more "Happy Holidays" from the lips of someone yearning to declare "Merry Christmas," or hear of one more lawsuit against a town with the audacity to place a nativity scene on public ground, I believe I will have to choose between screaming and crying. How about you?

That being said, I am not declaring a moratorium on gift-giving. The giving of gifts is a wonderful tradition and one that builds memories that last a lifetime. I am simply thinking aloud and wishing with all of my heart that those of us who call ourselves Christians could find it in our hearts to place Christ first during this season of celebration; that we who claim to be the "children of God" have the courage to declare "Merry Christmas" because of our unabashed love for Christ; that we put aside some of our worldly pursuits and worldly fears in favor of the things of God.

So celebrate the season with your families. Please don't neglect that. Buy too much if you wish. Eat too much if you must, but never forget what this season is all about. Never forget why we celebrate.

Christmas is a time to celebrate the coming of the Christ Child and all that that marvelous moment entails. This is the season to celebrate salvation coming to the earth in the person of Jesus Christ. We must be on guard that the miracle of the Christ Child is never overshadowed by the ways of the world, for that child came to this world of darkness to bring everlasting light and life eternal.

This Christmas season let us celebrate the Light! Celebrate the Life! Celebrate the coming of the Son of God into this world to bring us salvation from our sins! Celebrate the coming of the Son of God into this world to bring everlasting peace and joy! Celebrate the coming of the Son of God into this world to bring us His unconditional, everlasting love, which is beyond price! Celebrate it and pass it on! Merry Christmas.

For Christmas: Marvel

I will never forget my first Christmas as a married man. Mary and I were living in an 8x36-foot trailer in Lexington, South Carolina, at the time. I had lived in that thing with a cat named Charlie all the way through college, and it was just the right size for the cat. Nonetheless, we were happy as two bugs in a rug, as they say. We got ourselves a Christmas tree, piled some furniture up on the top of itself so we would have a place to put it, and then we realized we had no ornaments, no lights, and no money whatsoever. That being said, we determined that, reality aside, one way or the other we were going to get that tree decked out right even if it killed us. So we found a couple of pennies to rub together down in between the cushions of the sofa and headed to the first Kroger store that ever came to Columbia, the one over there on Bush River Road in a building that has since housed the Burlington Coat Factory and lots of other businesses. I believe that building has been torn down now and replaced with a Walmart. Time marches on, I suppose.

Well, we both were as excited as can be. After all, we were little more than kids ourselves. Mary had just turned twenty-one, and I was only four months ahead of her.

First of all, we got a couple of strands of lights, and then we took a look at the ornaments.

The first things we found were some of those glass ball ornaments; you know, the blue ones, the silver, and the red ones. Cheap, yeah, but we still have a couple of them forty years later. Of course, the paint is about gone from them, and the springy things have sprung, but we just can't bring ourselves to part with them.

After that first box of bobbles was purchased, we went treasure hunting. What we found were four blue bells with silver sparkles on them. We had to have them. They were the things of which heirlooms were made. So we decided that beans would be OK for a week or so and bought them. When we hung them on that tree, they

255

glistened and were just about the prettiest things we had ever seen.

When Christmas morning came that year, I do not remember a thing I received. I do remember those bells, however, and to this day as we continue the tradition of hanging those bells on our tree, I remember the innocence and the joy of that first Christmas with Mary. I remember all of the Christmases since, and I thank God for the joy of it all. I thank Him for the gift He has given me of a godly woman, three wonderful children, and seven beautiful grandchildren. I am amazed at His generosity to a man who gives so little in return. God is good, isn't He?

I will also never forget my first Christmas as a father. Sarah was all of four months old, and Mary and I were both still a bit scared of her, but we were going to do it right, you know.

We were living in Gilbert by that time in an old house that we were in the process of fixing up. Well, actually at that time we were in the process of making it habitable. Habitable or not, it was ours, and we didn't have to turn sideways to pass one another in the hall anymore, which is a strangely satisfying blessing if you have ever been there.

It was a really cold winter that year. In that we had no heat but a woodstove, it was a bit chilly in the house, but it was Christmas, we were young and in love, and the weather meant nothing to us. We were living in just one room of the house, because the stove would only heat that room. Yes, it was a bit cramped, but it was ours, and we had just been given a wonderful gift, the gift of life and family.

Christmas morning dawned, and Sarah kept on sleeping. I don't know why, but I figured a kid, even a four-month-old kid, would know it was Christmas and come a-running, but she just kept sleeping. Finally, Mary woke her up and sat her by the tree. She just sat there staring at the lights and the presents, as few as they were, marveling; and once again, I thanked God for my life, my family, and His love.

Since that time, I have had first Christmases nine more times, and each and every time the kid just sits there and marvels, and I know how they feel.

When I think of Christmas and its true meaning—I mean when I truly think of what happened on that starlit night, of the gift that was given—I am left speechless and amazed, and all I can do is marvel.

As this Christmas season dawns, make sure you take the time to marvel, as well.

Merry Christmas!

For Valentine's Day:
Love, True Love

I have struggled with what I should write this month. I've been dealing with one of the nastier bugs that has been making the rounds lately, and I think I may have strained my brain a bit during one of my coughing fits. No matter how hard I try, nothing is springing from that fountain of imagination that is usually so reliable.

My gray matter has gone black. The synaptic thunderstorm in my mind has become more of a gentle rain shower, nice for cozying up to the fire and pondering the simpler things of life, but not so great for writing an engaging and thought-provoking article.

So what to do? What to do? Listen to your wife, that's what.

"It's February," she said, "Write about love. You know the sappy, soppy, slushy type of love that you men claim you don't like."

So I figured, why not? So here it goes. Some scattered thoughts on love.

Love has a screw loose. It is downright crazy, isn't it? It ought to be fitted for a straightjacket. It hits you like a ton of bricks, and it completely takes you over. You can't sleep. You can't think. You just sit there and moon.

I seem to recall a young man back in the seventies who would drive a 150-mile round trip each and every week in a 1964 Valiant with no air, no heat, no speedometer, and not much of a roof just so he could be with his love. Sometimes he would make the trip twice just to see a ballet she was in—and trust me when I say that is true love.

Love is nuts. True love is virtuous insanity, but it is insanity nonetheless.

When you find that certain someone, reason takes a hike and mental illness and emotional instability move right on in. Y'all stop me if I get off track. I mean, what wouldn't you do for the ones you love?

Just saying it, if it's real, is never enough. It isn't so much that the lover needs to see some tangible evidence, as much as it is that the lovee needs to display something tangible.

If you love somebody, I mean really love somebody, you want the world to know it and see it. Am I right?

Love is a thousand yellow ribbons. It's Marvin Gaye singing, "Ain't no mountain high enough." Love is a single red rose resting in a crystal vase sitting on a sidewalk in mid-February. Love is never leaving, always caring, and being true. That is what true love looks like, isn't it?

Love is kissing your daughter's tears away and hiding yours when the time comes to give her away. Love is enduring a sixth-grade orchestra concert, a third-grade choir, and the heartbreak of a losing season. Love holds through thick and thin, sick and well, young and old, good times and bad.

Love sleeps all night on a little girl's floor just to make sure the monster is dead, and love gently brushes the hair of the woman who doesn't know your name but forever remains a part of you.

Love is a mountaintop where everything is possible, and love is a heartache so desolate only God above can offer comfort.

Love is a gift. Love is a curse. Love is life with all its glory and loss, all its joy and sorrow. Love is the marrow, the essence, the substance of life. Love is life.

"Whoever lives in love lives in God, and God in him" (1 John 4:16 NIV).

The author and his wife, Mary

For Valentine's Day:
Love Expressed

How is love expressed? Lots of ways, I suppose.

My granny had no shortage of ways of showing her love for me: a hug, a kiss on the cheek, teaching me how to bait a hook and hold my mouth just right while fishing, and an old King James Bible given to me at age seven. It was one of those smallish, zip-up black Bibles with a little bronze cross for a handle and great colored pictures inside. I never could quite figure out what King James was saying, but the pictures were marvelous. They gave me something to do during preaching.

Granny also demonstrated her love for me through a whupping or two, or three or more, to help me adjust this or that attitude that might come back to bite me one day. On top of that, she was an expert at trapping me with my own words and giving me an object lesson or two to get her point across.

From sending me to a shuttered market a mile down the road to fetch an ice-cold Coca-Cola on a ninety-five-degree Sabbath so I would learn to respect that day, to taking all my fish off the stringer and dropping them back into Whiskey Slough to teach me to quit complaining, she had her ways.

If it weren't for Granny's love and her unique way of teaching me lessons, though, I have no idea where I would be today.

Nowhere good, I suppose.

There are lots of ways of letting someone know you love them. No two ways are the same. They are unique to you and the one you love.

Lay your old army coat over her pretty shoulders on a cold October evening, and she'll be yours for life.

Shoot, if you're really good, you can ask for your allowance and express your love at the same time, kinda like a two for one deal.

Good Morning, Babe!

My dear, might you have a dollar or two
To spare for this dear old husband of you?
In lieu of a dollar, a check will do.
And never forget, I so do love you!

On tomorrow I'll be in Florence, you see,
And dinner is needed for others and me.
It may be hamburgers or fish from the sea,
And preacher or no, lunch is not free.

If you do have a dollar or dime in your purse,
Or not, please don't worry, I will not be terse.
I'll carry on 'neath no burden or curse,
For from your sweet love, I slake both hunger and thirst.

Love, Tony

I got the dollar, and I just might get an earful when this gets printed.

Like I said, though, there is no shortage of ways to let a loved one know how you feel about them. Whoever you love, I mean with that special love, let them know. I know they know, but they want to hear it. They need to hear it, and whether you want to admit it or not, so do you. Life is long; don't let them wonder. Tell them you love them. Life is short. Tell them today—don't wait!

I was going to get all theological on you, but sometimes we simply need to appreciate the gifts our Lord has given us. Take the time to appreciate your family. Take the time to appreciate the close friends you have. Take the time to truly appreciate that special someone with whom you have been blessed. Take the time to appreciate and cherish one of the greatest gifts to come down from heaven above.

Take the time to love.

For Easter:
Those Eyes

I will never forget the expression on her face. I wish I could find a way to describe it. It's been thirty-some odd years now, and I can still see her eyes just as plain as if it was yesterday. Black as onyx, filled with young life, and yet haunted somehow. Unforgettable, that's for sure. In all of my life, I don't think I have ever seen anything as lovely or as awful as those eyes. They filled me with hope and dread at the same time. Now how do you do that?

She was staring off into space with that newborn on her lap. She looked like she knew something no one else did. Yeah, I know all new mommas look kinda like that, but there was something else, something that gave her a wonderfully secretive smile, and Lord have mercy did that smile set off the tears in her eyes. Never has there been nor ever will there be anything more beautiful or more tragic than those eyes. I will never forget them. They've haunted me for more than thirty years now.

Oh, I've kept up the best I could over the years. I mean, it ain't every day a bunch of angels tell you where to go. That kind of thing sticks in your mind, you know. Not to mention seeing the baby, but it was those eyes, those eyes that captured me somehow.

I remember praying for that little girl as I headed home that evening, praying that she could find some peace somewhere, find something to take that terrible sorrow from her eyes.

I understand her boy has gotten Himself in some trouble as of late, started speaking the truth. Young'uns, they'll do that sometimes. It takes a bit of livin' to understand the truth makes folks uncomfortable. Heck, it makes 'em mad. It threatens 'em more often than not, especially a truth like His, but He was sent to tell them, so tell them He did.

I'm just glad I wasn't there to witness the kangaroo court and the beatings. Just watching them raise up that middle cross and drop it into place from a distance was enough to tear me up. The sound of that cross dropping carried all across the city. It rang out like an angry clap of thunder. It broke my heart, as old as I am. Even the sheep fell silent around me.

It rained all that day and on into the evening. About sunset, things calmed down a little, and by nightfall all was quiet—all but my mind, that is.

I couldn't sleep to save my soul that night. Every time I lay down, my mind would return to those haunted eyes from years before. Only now the smile had faded, and the tears of sorrow and pain were all that lingered.

It's been three days now since they pulled Him off that cross, and I slept pretty good last night. I just got up once or twice. I can tell you this, though—I do believe I saw the prettiest sunrise I have ever seen this morning, not a cloud in the sky. I hope His momma was up early enough to see it.

Have a blessed Easter.

Bolivian Praise, Ixiamas, Bolivia, by Tony Rowell

For Easter:
The Hunt

Over the years I have had folks ask me, "What in the world made you this way?"

I have never been quite sure how I should take that. So in keeping with my mother's philosophy of life, if the underlying motive for the question is not quite clear, I simply assume that the questioner is amazed at the quality folk standing before them and are wondering how to emulate such a thing. Now, that being said, if it's apparent that the question stems from neither fascination nor appreciation, I simply say, "Hey, don't blame me; my mother raised me!"

Let me expand on that a bit.

My mother, Bobbie Jean Rowell by name, was but a wisp of a woman. She reached one hundred pounds only when she was expecting me, and she was none too happy about that. She was a soft Southern belle, born and raised in the South, and like all proper Southern Belles she never wore white after Labor Day. With that being said, as many a Southern man has learned the hard way about Southern girls, that soft, demure exterior belied a core of spring steel and rawhide you had best not mess with if you knew what was good for you.

She was also a bit of a traditionalist in an unconventional, nontraditional way. This oddity in her makeup resulted in an Easter egg hunt that remains in my memory even though I was only four or five years old at the time. We were down on the panhandle of Florida visiting Granny and Grandpa Tharpe during the Easter break, and I wanted to go fishing while my mother wanted to have an Easter egg hunt for my brother and me.

Personally, at that time in my life at least, finding a hardboiled egg, colored up or not, did not even compare to watching a brightly colored cork head south with some poor unsuspecting fish on the other end of the line. Besides, the fun is in the coloring, not the finding, anyway.

Now, for those of you in the know, a determined five-year-old with a specific aim in mind can make your life miserable until you give in. I was told it was Easter and that fishing was forbidden, but I knew it was the day before Easter, so that didn't wash. I was told Granny had a lot of cooking to do, but I didn't care if it was Granny, Grandpa, or cousins John, Joan, and Jenny who went with me, I just wanted to go. I was told I was being childish, and that made perfect sense to me. I was five, after all. As it turned out, nothing could dissuade me, and my mother, spring steel and rawhide aside, gave in under the assault, or so it appeared.

Actually, she had a bit of Solomon in her and told me that we could all go fishing, all the way down at Willis Landing, if I would let us stop somewhere on the way and have an Easter egg hunt. It took me many years and a couple of kids of my own to admit that my mother had the whole thing planned and snookered me, a poor defenseless five-year-old.

So we piled in the old station wagon, clamped the fishing poles up on the roof, and headed off for Willis Landing: worms, crickets, and Easter eggs along for the ride. I kept asking Mom where we were going for the Easter egg hunt, by now my interest was piqued, and her only reply was, "We'll know when we get there." About an hour later, after we had made the right turn at Wewa and were heading east toward Port St. Joe and Willis Landing, Mom whispered something in Grandpa's ear and he hit the brakes, did a three-point turn, and headed back the other way.

By now I was craning my neck to see out the window, excited to find out where we were going. As we turned into an old driveway, I saw what had to be the perfect place for a couple of young adventurous boys to have an Easter egg hunt. We both rolled out of the car and were confronted with an old dilapidated house. The yard was littered with all sorts of wonderful things to plunder. There was an old wringer-washer, and an old icebox—not an Igloo, mind you, but a genuine icebox with wooden sides and all. There was an old rusted car and enough junk scattered around to keep a couple of pickers in business for a year. It was beautiful. My mother had hit a home run in my eyes.

After Grandpa had gone through the place with a big stick making enough noise to wake the dead and shoo away any critter with untoward designs on his grandchildren, the eggs were hidden and Mike, my older brother, and I had the time of our lives plundering without having to worry about getting caught.

In retrospect, I honestly cannot remember if we even went fishing that day. I know we did though, because my Momma might out smart a five-year-old, but she would never lie to one.

Now why do I tell this story?

Well, now that I am beyond being a mere parent and have entered into the grandparent stage of life, I can look back at this story from so many years ago and be honest with myself. I can look back at that Easter egg hunt with the realization that my five-year-old mind had falsely convinced me I was in control of the situation. All I wanted was to go fishing, but my mother had greater plans for me that spring afternoon sometime back in the early sixties.

Upon reflection I know now that, had I gotten my way back then and not been bamboozled by my mother, I would never have found the Easter egg resting in that old Ford Fairlane fender, and I would not have kept this memory with me all these years. A memory that brings with it just a hint of childhood and the faint aroma of my mom, an enchanting mixture of Dove soap, Chanel No. 5, and sweetness.

Expanding upon that thought, I can look back at unnumbered other times when I had convinced myself I was in charge of my destiny, that my decisions and my wants were paramount, only to realize later that a greater intellect with a greater purpose for me was gently prodding me forward toward heights I could have never imagined.

I remain convinced to this day that our Lord and Savior has a plan, a wonderfully meaningful plan, for each and every one of His followers. I am convinced He has beautiful plans for His church. It is my prayer that we as followers of Christ can learn to release the grasp we so resolutely, and might I say childishly, hold upon our destinies long enough to realize how foolish we are to think we are in control.

I am also convinced that this realization, and the resulting freedom it will bring as we give control over to Christ, promises to open up the storehouse of heaven so that the blessings of our Lord and Savior Jesus Christ can rain down upon His people and take us to heights we can only imagine.

The author, as a child, with his mother.

For Easter:
The Morning

It was early, sometime between the dark of night and the grayish purple of beginning dawn. A thin veil of silver mist covered the hillside as a few deer ventured out for one last time before bedding down for the day. The mockingbirds were giving over the night to the morning larks, and the stars were quickly fading in the face of the coming sun.

As I began trying to envision the morning when the stone rolled away and my resurrected Lord stepped from the tomb, I wanted to draw you, the reader, into the scene. I wanted you to smell, to feel, to hear, to be part of the moment when the world's shackles fell away. I truly wanted you to hear the rustling grass as the early-morning field mice started at the sound of resurrected feet taking their first step. I wanted you to stare in silent wonder at the white breath of the Christ hanging suspended on the cold morning air. I wanted to make it real, so real that you could not deny.

I wished to make it so you trembled in fear as the earth shook under your feet when the covering stone rolled back, watching, muted, as winged lightning opened the floodgates of eternity. Listening as the heavenly being proclaimed the end of death and the birth of life.

Feeling, with the women, the heart-stopping fear, all the while hearing, "Do not be afraid!" Hearing without comprehension of promises kept, of prophecies fulfilled, of love in full bloom.

I wanted your ears to hear "Greetings" from beyond the grave. I wished for your hands to clasp His feet and for your lips to kiss the stain away. I longed for your fingers to explore the torn pathway of the spike, tracing its course on its way to the cross. And I longed, make that I long, for you to know the Truth.

I yearn for you to leave empirical knowledge on the shelf long enough to grasp a Truth that goes far beyond our limited ability to understand.

For Christ is Truth, and His love is true.

Easter morning celebrates His love and the promise of eternity it brings.

This Easter morning, I pray you rest in Christ's peace and celebrate His everlasting love.

Index

Granny and Grandpa Stories

Mission Stories

Family Stories

Hiking/Fishing/Nature Stories

Legacy Stories

This and That Stories

Southern Places Stories

Special Days Stories

About the Author

Anthony S. "Tony" Rowell was born in Circleville, Ohio, to Bill and Bobbe Rowell. As a young child, he and his family moved up and down the East Coast from Upstate New York to Florida, and he got to spend many happy summers with his grandparents in Panama City, Florida. His family settled in South Carolina during his teen years, which was also when he truly came to know Christ. Through music ministry and mission work, Tony realized his call to full-time ministry in 1993. He has served as both vice chair and chair of the United Methodist Volunteers in Mission in South Carolina and has pastored seven churches. He is a photographer, songwriter, guitarist, and cabinetmaker. Tony is married to his high school sweetheart, Mary, and they have three grown children and seven grandkids, all of whom are good-looking, talented, and highly intelligent.

Rowell

CPSIA information can be obtained
at www.ICGtesting.com
Printed in the USA
FSHW012158050620
70784FS